A MINER'S LAMP
AND A BRASS TABLE

A MINER'S LAMP AND A BRASS TABLE

A Yorkshire Reporter's Story

GUY WILLIAMS

Published by Guy Williams

A CIP catalogue record for this book is available from the British Library.

ISBN 978-1-5262-0986-3

Book layout and cover design by Clare Brayshaw

Prepared and printed by:

York Publishing Services Ltd
64 Hallfield Road
Layerthorpe
York YO31 7ZQ

Tel: 01904 431213

Website: www.yps-publishing.co.uk

CONTENTS

FOREWORD
BY SIR IAN MCGEECHAN OBE

I have to be thankful for a Yorkshire mother, born in Morley, near Leeds, and a Scottish father, and, apparently, my mother making it quite clear, when they married, that life would be in Yorkshire.

What was so influential to my younger brother and me was that they both loved sport. Football and cricket dominated our upbringing – football at Elland Road and Test match cricket after school at Headingley, and then played every night in the street.

Over the years I have spoken to Guy at so many different events and occasions, mostly, I would have to admit, linked with rugby, but also, at times, on Yorkshire cricket, a sport we both follow and enjoy immensely.

Guy has a knowledge and understanding of all sport, especially when it relates directly to a Yorkshire team, but more importantly how sport relates, in a very special way to its environment.

I have to admit to a certain bias, but sport is so much part of what Yorkshire is, and the social characteristics which bred a competiveness and stubbornness to compete from early years to adulthood.

Guy's writing brings out that very uniqueness of a Yorkshire spirit both on the sports field and away from it.It is why I have always enjoyed reading his pieces, he merges character with actions and highlights those special feelings which come with victory and defeat.

I am sure, as you read his stories, you will feel the Yorkshire spirit which has driven many of us in so many different ways.

Sir Ian McGeechan OBE.
Head Coach British and Irish Lions 1989, 1993, 1997 and 2009

ACKNOWLEDGEMENTS

Sir Ian McGeechan, Clare Brayshaw (York Publishing), David Frith (cricket pictures), Brian Sanderson (cricket pictures), Jeremy Lonsdale (cricket pictures), The Cricketer, Humber Bridge Board, RNLI and Spurn Kilnsea and Easington Area Local Studies, Kingston Communications, The Cricket Paper, The Rugby Paper, Rotherham Titans RUFC, Doncaster Knights RUFC, Marisa Cashill (The Yorkshire Post), Danielle Wiles (Parliamentary Archives), British and Irish Lions, Norman Allen, Giggleswick School, Andrew White (Northern Echo), Michael Temple (Notts CCC), Amber Lewis (RFU), Andrew Mosley (Rotherham Advertiser), George Harbey (Nottingham Forest FC), Sinn Fein Press Office, Graham Ironside (ex-Yorkshire Television), Liberal Democrats Press Office, Ye Olde White Harte, Hull, St. Andrews Dock Heritage Action Group (Hull), Hull Daily Mail, The Deep (Hull), John Ashton, Doncaster Knights photographer and The Barnsley Branch of the National Union of Mineworkers.

ABOUT THE AUTHOR

Guy Williams has been a journalist for more than 50 years, working for the BBC, Yorkshire Television and for national and regional newspapers.

Educated at Giggleswick School near Settle in North Yorkshire and at Liverpool University, Guy writes for The Rugby Paper, The Cricket Paper, The Cricketer and The Yorkshire Post and its magazine.

He is married to Liane and lives in Barkston Ash near Tadcaster.

INTRODUCTION

I'm very lucky to have so many close friends, many of whom have said I should write a book based on the stories I've told over a few drinks. I wasn't sure at first, but the more I thought about it, the more it became a good idea, particularly as my children, Tommy and Laura, may not be too aware as to how their father earned a living. My wife, too, Liane should know in some detail what I did as a reporter before we married in 2010, and my two grandchildren, Rupert and Arabella, also I'd like to think, would be interested to read what their grandfather did professionally.

As I write Rupert and Arabella are living in Doha in Qatar which makes it difficult to establish the same sort of close relationship I had with my grandparents, and while WhatsApp and Zoom can bring you together, it's not quite the same as having your grandchildren in the same country or within driving distance.

Having said that they are now living in Devon, so contact is much easier.

Therefore, with the family background that we share, I wanted to write my story so that you'll eventually get to know your grandpa and his role as a journalist in radio, television, newspapers and magazines.

This account is being put together, for the most part, in the spring and summer of 2020, and in the early months of 2021, during the Coronavirus Crisis, the most serious threat to life in the UK and beyond since the Second World War between 1939-45.

Indeed, by May 2022, the number of people who'd died from Covid had reached more than 175,000 in the UK since the original outbreak in the early months of 2020.

As the country ground to halt, normal everyday life as we'd known it, in my case for more than 70 years, ended.

For example, I could no longer work as usual as a reporter for The Yorkshire Post, a distinguished paper whose origins began in 1754, covering rugby union and writing features called My Yorkshire for the paper's magazine published on Saturdays.

As well as that, I also wrote for a national publication, The Rugby Paper. My job here was to cover games involving two clubs in South Yorkshire, Doncaster Knights and Rotherham Titans, who played in national competitions on Saturdays. My reports would appear in The Yorkshire Post on Mondays and on Sundays in The Rugby Paper.

As the Coronavirus Crisis worsened, match reporting discontinued as rugby's governing body, the Rugby Football Union, cancelled the rest of the season affecting the leagues I covered. Under normal circumstances, I would have gone on immediately the rugby season finished in late April or early May to write features on Yorkshire cricket for The Cricket Paper, another national publication. But as with all other sport, both professional and amateur, first class cricket was suspended until it was safe to resume (behind closed doors with no spectators), so longish features on Yorkshire players and issues could not be written because the paper ceased publication until it resumed in August.

So with regular newspaper work ending, in my case for the first time in 30 years, I thought it might be of interest to my friends and grandchildren to write a book.

Before I explain the title, which refers to my past relations, my grandparents were from Yorkshire and Lancashire, I'd like to point out that everything I've written for a variety of national and provincial papers and magazines has been kept.

One of the great joys and thrills of being a journalist is seeing your work published. By the time you are old enough to understand the media, no doubt another revolution in reporting will have taken place, but in my era newspapers, while in decline, remained popular.

The Age of the Internet rules as I write, but to show how your grandfather earned a living most enjoyably, in another generation, I have kept more than 60 scrapbooks containing cuttings from papers already mentioned plus The Sunday Times, The Observer, The Independent on Sunday, News of the World and The Sun, all national papers. In addition, I wrote for The Star in Sheffield and its sports paper, The Green 'Un, which used to be published only on a Saturday shortly after football matches had finished.

I also had much pleasure writing for a rugby magazine, The Cricketer, Wisden Cricket Monthly and Sports Illustrated, based in Cape Town, South Africa.

As you'll find out, I also worked in broadcast journalism and some of my reports for Yorkshire Television are recorded on a CD.

If you both have as much fun in your careers as I have, you'll be extremely happy and, as a result, I hope most successful.

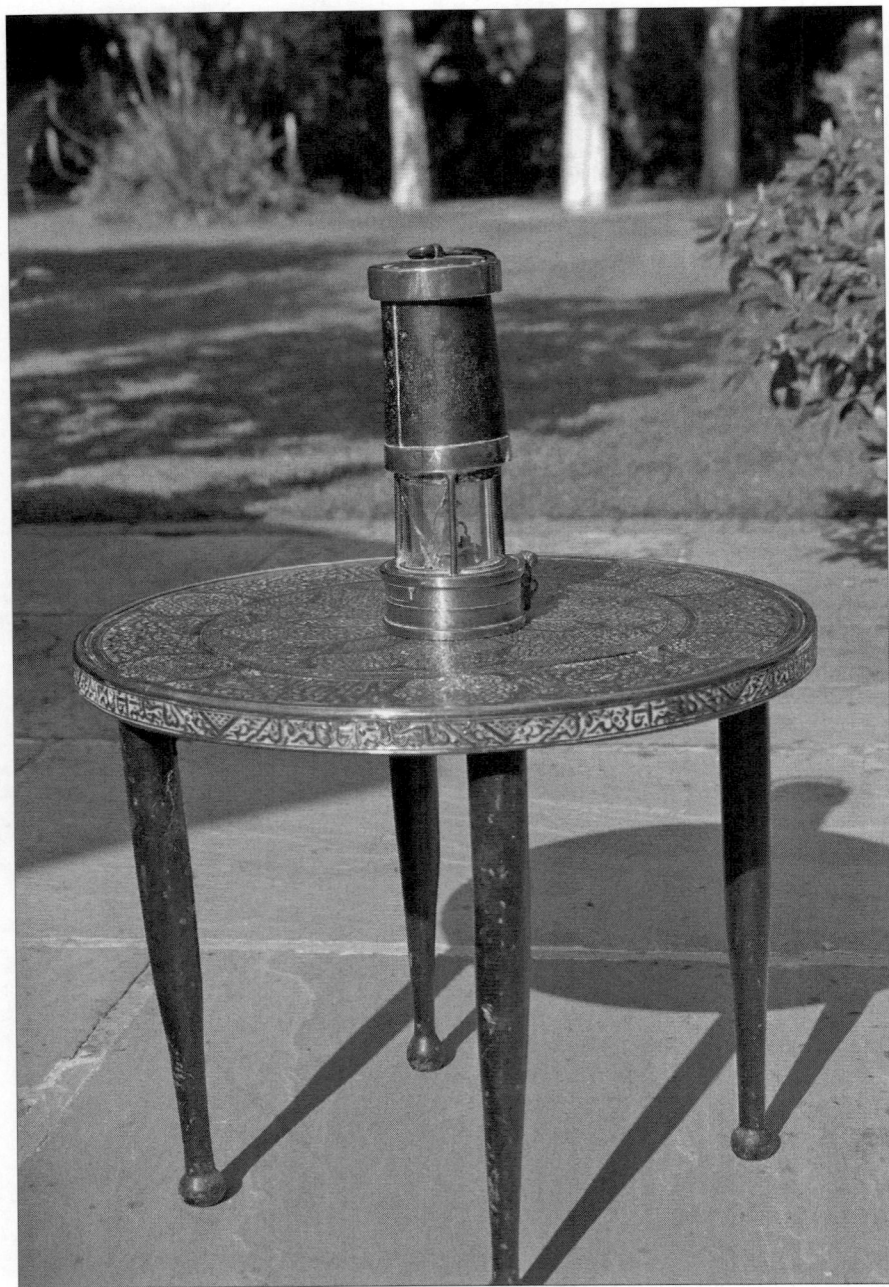

CHAPTER ONE

WHY A MINER'S LAMP
AND A BRASS TABLE?

Family possessions help to define who you are and they are among my favourite and are and were part of the furniture at homes I've lived in. I've always felt an emotional attachment to the miner's lamp and to the brass table because each tells a story relating to the Williams family. Both belonged to different sections of my relatives, all of whom grew up and lived in the North of England, and in particular Lancashire and Yorkshire.

The Victorian brass miner's lamp is, I believe, from the 1870s, and was given to me by my uncle John on his retirement in the early 1960s from his pit at Maltby near Rotherham where he worked as a safety manager. Your generation will learn of the importance of British coal mining; how significant its role was in providing power to manufacturing as the Industrial Revolution gathered pace. The railways in the era of steam locomotives were fuelled by coal as was the production of electricity. Your studies will also inform you that coal provided the power for the Royal Navy as it protected the Empire.

My lamp, invented by Sir Humphrey Davy in 1815 to detect explosive gasses underground so that miners had a better chance of escaping death, will have experienced extreme danger, but provided a measure of safety to workers digging for coal in one of the most lethal industries in the country.

Uncle John, my godmother's father, was employed as a pit deputy whose job was to enforce mine safety regulations in an industry which, like steam locos, now belongs to history books.

Ever since I saw a picture of a bare chested coal miner from the 1920s in a school book of my mother's, I've had a natural sympathy for mining communities, not in a patronising way, but rather an understanding of the hardships they faced and an appreciation of the importance, industrially and politically, coal played in the nation's affairs.

As mentioned earlier, I've enjoyed covering sport, and mining areas in the UK have produced many outstanding sportsmen and women who have achieved national and international fame.

In my career, for example, I've done stories with footballers Sir Bobby and Jack Charlton who grew up in the North East at Ashington, once described as the biggest mining village in the country; their achievements at Manchester United and Leeds United were quite brilliant but their biggest triumph was winning the World Cup for England in 1966.

And when it comes to the sports I've covered most, rugby union and cricket, the pit villages of South Wales were the breeding grounds for many Welsh and British and Irish Lions internationals, such as Cliff Morgan from the 1950s and Sir Gareth Edwards in the 1960s and 70s. As regards Yorkshire cricketers I've known, Fred Trueman for instance, the great Yorkshire and England fast bowler, the first bowler to take 300 Test wickets, who grew up near Maltby, and Dickie Bird, who became the world's best Test umpire, lived in Barnsley. His father worked down the pit for more than 50 years.

Later on, there'll be more details about cricket and cricketers and the personal memories I have, but the toughness, strength and resilience showed by sportsmen and women from mining backgrounds helped make them so competitive. Politically miners were also most influential and you had to be hard to survive underground.

In the years before and after the Second World War, miners' leaders, such as Sam Watson, the boss of Durham National Union of Mineworkers, were powerful figures in the Labour Party, and as the post war era developed, were politically close to Clem Attlee, Prime Minister between 1945-51.

Early in my career as a reporter at BBC Radio Leicester, I frequently interviewed Frank Smith, the moderate leader of the small coalfield in Leicestershire, and when I moved to work in London at the BBC newsroom in Broadcasting House, the headquarters of the BBC, I remember clearly two occasions which involved the then president of the NUM, Joe Gormley, a warm and level headed Lancastrian from the Wigan area.

He was, though, a tough negotiator who led the national strike in 1972, and when the NUM called another strike two years later, the miners, in effect, were responsible for toppling the Conservative Prime Minister, Ted Heath.

During the mid-1970s, I attended a press conference in London at what was then the HQ of the NUM on Euston Road. Before mobile phones and other digital gadgets, demanding news desks were unable to speak to reporters instantly. But communication pagers were available. Instead of switching mine off so the alarm signal from the news desk wouldn't go off, I foolishly left it on.

Joe Gormley made life peer in 1982

The loud noise brought Gormley's statement to a halt. Joe was not amused and burst out: "What the f…k is that?"

Embarrassed, I turned the alarm off, fearing I wouldn't get the interview my bosses needed. However, Gormley, after speaking to national correspondents, was quite happy to be interviewed, so I got my story.

But a few weeks later, I almost failed to supply the story that had been ordered by a BBC news programme. I was late leaving the newsroom and arrived at the NUM HQ at least 20 minutes late for my appointment. As I entered the building, Joe Gormley was walking out of the lift.

I apologised and was anxious that I'd missed an important story. However, Joe couldn't have been kinder or more understanding.

"Don't worry lad. Get your tape recorder out and we can do it now."

A keen, young reporter was rather relieved and before Joe, one of the most powerful men in the UK, wearing his trademark dark overcoat and black hat, left the premises, he nodded, winked and crunched my hand saying: "I like to look after you lads."

The next prominent miners' leader I reported on was arguably the most controversial trade union figure in the UK post war: Arthur Scargill who led the year long national strike during 12 bitter and bloody months from March 1984 until the following March.

Arthur Scargill

Scargill, a Marxist, held political beliefs which were far removed from Gormley's; nevertheless he had widespread support in his own coalfield, Yorkshire, and Scargill's oratory and clever use of the media, particularly television, turned him into a formidable opponent of the then Prime Minister, Margaret Thatcher, whose style during the strike was as rigid as Scargill's.

Being a journalist at Yorkshire Television in Leeds meant that the newsroom was right in the thick of things, broadcasting daily on an often violent strike which affected thousands of our viewers in the region. Every effort was made to be strictly fair in our reporting, so that both sides, the Thatcher Government/National Coal Board (employers) and the NUM were covered accurately.

That's not to say that complaints were not made. I recall taking an angry phone call from the Left Wing Labour MP, Dennis Skinner, who represented the mining constituency of Bolsover in Derbyshire.

I recognised his voice as soon as I picked up the phone:

"I'd like to speak to the bugger who wrote the miners' story I've just watched on your lunchtime news."

"You are speaking to him," I replied.

"Well, it's not right and please ask your boss, Graham Ironside, to ring me as soon as possible."

I am not sure what assurances, if any, were given by YTV's head of news, but, in difficult editorial circumstances, he would have repeated the company's policy that impartiality and accuracy were the standards Yorkshire Television demanded.

As regards Scargill, a witty man in private and a high class mimic, he and I shared an amusing moment at the height of the strike called to stop pit closures.

I remember interviewing Scargill in his office at the NUM HQ which had moved to Sheffield. After we had chatted about the points both of us were going to make, the cameraman said: "Off you go Guy."

As I said: "Mr Scargill thanks for your time…"

My question was interrupted by Scargill's laughter. The reason? As I asked the question, I moved slightly across my leather chair and in the process it sounded if I'd farted loudly.

We both saw the funny side, proving to me that this driven and dedicated Marxist, hated by Daily Mail and Daily Telegraph readers and opposed by Neil Kinnock, the Leader of the Labour Party, had at least a sense of humour.

After completing the interview about the chances of a settlement, there were none, Scargill and I chatted about less controversial matters. Knowing that he'd started work underground, aged 15, soon after leaving school, we talked about the possibility of doing a feature after the strike at Woolley Colliery near Barnsley. In particular, I wanted to put together a story which showed Arthur Scargill in another light, and definitely not the Scargill who ranted and shouted while on the picket line or addressing through a loudhailer hundreds of cheering, striking miners.

"What do you have in mind?"

"How about a story that shows you being reunited with the pit pony you looked after at Woolley pit?"

"I'd love that. The pony's still about and in a field near the colliery, I think."

Sadly, we never got round to it, a missed opportunity I am afraid, and inevitably as the strike continued, the bitterness directed at Margaret Thatcher grew and grew in the mining communities where pits were the main employers.

How families in the Yorkshire coalfield principally in the Wakefield, Barnsley, Doncaster and Rotherham areas were trapped in the dispute on opposing sides, was emphasised to me when early one morning I covered the return to work of a handful of miners to a pit in Glasshoughton near Castleford.

Dozens of police lined the approach to the pit as returning miners were driven rapidly in hurtling vans, covered in protective grilles, towards the pit entrance. As the striking miners shouted abuse at the scabs (strike breakers), the senior police officer in charge walked across to ask which television company we were from.

"Yorkshire Television", I said.

"Well, you can tell your viewers that I'm in an awkward position. I'm from a mining family. My brother's on strike and I've got to uphold the law. Life's a bit difficult."

More than 40 years since the end of the strike, trade union militancy has been crushed, although the unions representing railway workers and NHS staff caused widespread disruption in 2023. Mining communities, once dominated by pit head gear, have been transformed; familiar features common over many decades to previous generations have been turned into supermarkets, restaurants, cinemas, a dry ski slope and dozens of small and medium size businesses on industrial estates. Alternative jobs have been provided which are much safer.

The brass Davy lamp, which looks golden when highly polished, stands for many things, I believe.

It's essential to understand the importance of this country's industrial history and the significance of inventions; the lamp represents a past, often bitter and deadly, and because it belongs to yesterday, there has to be a tomorrow. This country has a moral duty, I argue, to ensure that future generations enjoy rising prosperity and first class public services in those communities which lost their identity and may be searching to establish a new one.

CHAPTER TWO

THE BRASS TABLE

The Davy lamp belongs firmly in Yorkshire where one side of your family originated. For example, my maternal grandfather, Edward Larrad, lived in Huddersfield and traded in the finest cloth, the West Riding employed thousands in the textile industry.

However, the brass table's home was across the Pennines; mountains and hills running down the North of England from Northumberland to Derbyshire.

The table's roots are Lancastrian and especially from Manchester and its surrounding area, taking in Warrington and Liverpool. I was fortunate as a child to know both sets of grandparents, and the brass table was a familiar site in the Manchester home of Alfred and Mabel Williams, my father's parents.

Grandad Williams

Granny Williams

Grandad Williams, a large and generous man, held the top job in the Manchester and Salford Cooperative Society. Coop supermarkets today are somewhat different to the business which grandad ran in the 1950s. As general manager, he was responsible for one of the biggest retailers outside London. Unlike the present generation, grandad Williams stayed with the same employer for his entire working life, as did my father. After surviving the First World War (1914-18), in which he served as a stretcher bearer in the Royal Army Medical Corps in the battlefields of Thessalonika in Greece, his first job was at the Coop in Newport in South Wales.

Success earned promotion to a better paid job in Manchester where he remained until his retirement as general manager in the late 1950s.

What did I learn from grandad and granny Williams who trained as a teacher in Liverpool before the Great War?

The value of hard work and proof that if you work hard and enjoy good fortune, you can go far. In his case from the lowly status of his first job as a lather boy in a barber's shop(preparing shaving cream)to the leather chairs in the boardroom.

Grandad supported the Labour Party but was by no means a doctrinaire socialist. He combined a belief in social justice with his wish for a successful capitalist economy. He disliked snobbery and felt at home reading and appreciating the moderate left wing opinions advocated by the Manchester Guardian, later re-named The Guardian in 1959.

I suppose my love of newspapers was inspired by granny and grandad Williams. Granny, whose father was active in Liberal politics as a prominent councillor in Warrington, never seemed to be without a paper or book. The Williamses took the Manchester Guardian, the Manchester Evening News and the News Chronicle, a leftish paper which folded in 1960. Granny showed little interest in cooking and often read while trying to prepare a meal. Indeed, on one occasion the paper caught fire in the kitchen because all her attention was on an article rather than the contents of the pan.

Interestingly, my enthusiasm for putting and keeping everything I've written for national and provincial newspapers into scrapbooks must have been inherited from granny Williams' father, Ebenezer England, an accountant who performed a major municipal role in Warrington and served on Lancashire's Education Committee.

The collection of his cuttings, mainly before the Great War, not only tells you his personal history, but also covers national politics before the outbreak of the 14-18 War. The old cuttings book portrays an account of a period in this country's history which you will not be familiar with, but I think it's essential to know your family's background because you will share characteristics which your parents have and those of your grandparents and their grandparents too.

Grandad and granny Williams owned a house and a car in the 1930s when many families didn't because poverty and unemployment were widespread. They enjoyed a comfortable standard of living, took nothing for granted and stressed the importance of saving and not living beyond their means.

The owners of the brass table weren't reluctant to spend money or indeed catch up with the growing popularity of television. To own a television in the early 1950s was quite extraordinary and, indeed, a privilege. In grandad's case he'd bought a Murphy with a screen which, I think, was either 12 or 14 inches, certainly bigger than my uncle Roy's which was only nine.

Like millions, the first programme I watched was the Coronation of the Queen in June 1953. Grandad's living room was crowded because he'd also invited his neighbours to watch the coverage in black and white pictures, the first time this historic event and ancient ceremony had been broadcast on television.

It was seen by 27 million viewers in the UK which then had a population of 36 millions. Indeed, the Coronation was also the first major world event to be broadcast internationally. Attended by 8,000 guests in Westminster Abbey, many from the 129 nations represented; I can remember clearly more than 20 members of reigning royal families arriving, and in particular, Queen Salote of Tonga, a rather large lady who defied the rain by insisting on riding in an open carriage.

Across the Pennines, my other grandparents, living in a solid stone house in a village called Brockholes near Huddersfield, didn't own a telly, but granny and grandpa Larrad, a cloth merchant, gradually gave way and bought their first television in the late 1950s.

While I loved granny Larrad very much, grandpa in a quiet way was somewhat cold and hard; he didn't approve of my mother's marriage and

Grandpa Larrad

didn't attend the wedding towards the end of the Second World War. He believed she had married beneath her status, utter nonsense and an alien attitude to hold because I never detected snobbery or class consciousness by others on either side of the family.

Grandpa, though, was thoroughly professional and knew the value and quality of cloth. Born in Dewsbury, a textile mill town, not that far from Leeds, his knowledge and expertise provided a comfortable standard of living and made enough money to afford a private education for my mother in the 1930s which was uncommon.

Great Grandmother, Mother, Me (Guy) and Granny Larrad

Granny Larrad &
Great Grandmother

Granny Larrad

Granny Larrad, who also trained as a teacher before the First World War, did not have the happiest of marriages because grandpa was mean and instead of spending it on his wife preferred to help his brother and sister and their children.

The relative who stood out as I was growing up was granny Larrad's mother, my great grandmother, whom we called Big Granny. Tall and sliver haired, she never dressed in bright colours and always wore black or navy blue. Affectionate and Victorian in her manners and style, Nancy Rimmer was typical of her epoch and accustomed to regular Sunday worship. Like my grandparents from Manchester, who were Methodists and rarely, if ever, drank alcohol, Big Granny was also a Non-Conformist, but her church was something quite different, Particular Baptist. I'm not sure how you differentiate between Particular Baptists and other Baptists, but my great grandmother certainly knew which brand she liked and was driven to the chapel each Sunday morning in an elegant crimson car with a long bonnet and running boards by an equally smartly dressed gentleman called Mr. Lithgow.

Big Granny almost whispered as she spoke and being born in the 1860s represented a living history book. She talked about events and people I would soon learn about at school, and I recall her telling me that she remembered Queen Victoria (monarch between 1837-1901) opening the Manchester Ship Canal, one of the most important features of industrial activity in the North of England, in 1894.

More than 30 years later, I was reminded of my great grandmother and her era during a reporting stint in Sheffield for Yorkshire Television. It was a fascinating story to do because at the centre of it was an old lady celebrating her 100th birthday. Her bed was surrounded by cards, including one from the Queen, and as we chatted, she remembered accurately seeing Queen Victoria arriving in a horse drawn carriage at Sheffield Town Hall as the city marked her Diamond Jubilee in 1897.

What's more this lady showed me a book given to all Sheffield's school children so they would recall the special occasion, and to make it an even stronger story, Yorkshire Television's film research officer in London, after much digging, unearthed rare footage, 13 golden seconds taken in Sheffield showing the Queen's arrival and her being greeted by the city's Lord Mayor. There, clearly visible, was the Empress of India, a small plump monarch dressed in black whose visit to Sheffield, almost 100 years ago, was being described vividly by an articulate centenarian.

CHAPTER THREE

MOTHER AND FATHER

Landing a job at the BBC, first as a lowly local radio trainee at BBC Radio Leicester and then in other roles in London, followed by a reporter's position at Yorkshire Television, wouldn't have been possible without sacrifices made by my parents, Margaret and Freddie Williams.

Throughout his successful business career with the Dunlop Rubber Company, my father spent 40 years with the same employer which was common in the post war era. He rose progressively from a sales clerk in Manchester (1937 till war broke out) to being a director of one of Dunlop's main divisions on Tyneside where he achieved several Queen's Awards for technical achievement and export success.

The production of industrial hosepipe in the North East, Grimsby and at a factory near Liverpool took over his life, so there was little time for his favourite sports, hockey and tennis, which he had enjoyed before the war.

Popular on the shop floor and with union officials, dad's capacity for hard work produced good results which in turn led to regular promotions.

My father's partnership with my mother worked well. His salary for at least 10 years was supplemented by her jobs with the Yorkshire Electricity Board at Holmfirth near Huddersfield and then on Tyneside. Two incomes made it financially possible to educate me at three fee paying schools: in Holmfirth where one of my friends was Robert Newton whose uncle was the famous actor of the same name, secondly at Ramillies Hall, a prep school near Manchester, and finally at Giggleswick near Settle in the Yorkshire Dales.

While my enthusiasm for modern history, politics and newspapers was inspired by my grandparents, my abiding interest and love of sport, especially cricket, rugby and football (Huddersfield Town, Newcastle United, Sunderland and Liverpool) was forged at schools where the facilities were first class and the staff encouraging.

The sacrifices made by my parents had one major benefit – growing up as a late developer, I was spared the exacting demands of the 11 plus exam. My brain was not sharp enough to cope with the grammar school entrance test which I would have failed. Like other failures, I could have been educated at a secondary modern.

Mother & Father

I was spared that because I eventually matured academically at Giggleswick, achieved decent A level grades and studied Politics at Liverpool University.

Both Ramillies Hall and Giggleswick were attended by boys, mainly from the North, whose parents were fairly well off, but not super-rich or aristocratic. Public school snobbery was never a theme and I came across its offensive nature only when I was living and working in London and met people, employed in the City, who assumed they'd been to posher schools in the Midlands or the South.

Fortunate to love both schools, I rarely suffered home sickness and as a happy boarder I looked forward to returning at the end of the holidays.

The headmaster at Ramillies, Captain Kenneth Patterson, I liked and respected. He drove a Citroen, the first foreign car I saw, and, unusually for the late 1950s, was married to an Indian lady whose flowing, colourful saris somehow didn't seem out of place in the suburbs of Manchester.

Many of the boys were keen supporters of Manchester United, and we followed the exciting football played by the Busby Babes in the national and provincial press. I remember clearly hearing the devastating news of the Munich air disaster in February 1958 in which 23 people were killed, including eight United stars. Captain Patterson walked into my dormitory to tell us the horrific news. We were woken up and then he explained, as far as he knew, the details of the crash and then calmly asked if we had any questions.

I put my hand up: "Captain Patterson, how is Bobby Charlton?"

"Williams, I believe he has survived."

What more could he say? And with that reassuring but stunning news about the deaths of Charlton's team-mates, Patterson left the dormitory.

Eight newspaper reporters who'd covered the European Cup match against Red Star Belgrade also perished in the disaster, but miraculously against all the odds, Frank Taylor, reporting the match for the News Chronicle, survived.

Frank suffered terribly with severe injuries to his right leg and left arm. He never made a full recovery but went on to establish a distinguished career in Fleet Street (then the home of national newspapers) on the Daily Herald, The Sun and Daily Mirror. He also wrote a most moving book on the disaster titled: The Day a Team Died.

Frank Taylor on the right

Years later and to my amazement, I met Frank Taylor at a rugby union game in Wakefield, an unlikely setting for him, I was covering for The Sunday Times and The Yorkshire Post. After I phoned my copy through, Mr. Taylor, sitting near the press bench, approached me and said: "I used to do that when I was a football reporter."

Naturally, I was keen to find out more.

"Can we talk about it over a pint?"

As we strolled to the Wakefield clubhouse and the crowded bar, I noticed that Frank walked with a stick.

And it was in the College Grove bar that this experienced journalist, now retired, gradually explained what had happened

I listened in silence for what seemed hours as he recounted the names of the players who'd died…Geoff Bent, Roger Byrne, Eddie Coleman, Duncan Edwards, Mark Jones, David Pegg, Tommy Taylor and Billy Whelan and those of his colleagues in the press…Alf Clarke, Manchester Chronicle, Don Davies, Manchester Guardian, George Follows, Daily Herald, Archie Ledbrooke, Daily Mirror, Henry Rose, Daily Express, Frank Swift, News of the World, Eric Thompson, Daily Mail and Tom Jackson of the Manchester Evening News.

Frank also talked of the emotional recovery Manchester United made, inspired by manager Matt Busby, culminating famously in the club winning the European Cup 10 years after Munich.

It was a privilege to meet Frank Taylor and he left an impression on me that I will always remember fondly.

I've never covered football matches, although as a radio reporter (Leicester City) and journalist at YTV, I reported on many football news stories associated with the region's main clubs, for example, Leeds United, Sheffield Wednesday, Sheffield United, Huddersfield Town and Hull City. However, on leaving YTV in 1991, for a period I freelanced for the sports desk of Sky News.

One story in particular reminded me of the tragic events at Munich on Thursday February 6th 1958. Before a European match at Old Trafford, I was asked to preview the game and interview manager Alex Ferguson and the captain Bryan Robson.

To go with these interviews and library footage of recent European games involving Manchester United, I also needed shots of Old Trafford and suggested strongly to the cameraman they must include pictures of the Munich Clock commemorating the disaster.

The clock is mounted proudly at the south east corner of the stadium.

Munich clock at Old Trafford Football Stadium

Is there another more memorable feature at Old Trafford or one that is more emotional?

I was more than aware of it, but the cameraman, from another generation and ignorant of the clock's significance, required an explanation as to why our story should begin with this shot. Frank Taylor could have told him as could Bobby Charlton.

CHAPTER FOUR

GIGGLESWICK

O n reflection, my natural interest in politics and newspapers was unquestionably strengthened at Giggleswick School, founded during Tudor times in 1512. It's hard to think of any school which enjoys such a beautiful setting in the Yorkshire Dales. The magnificent school chapel, opened in 1901 to commemorate Queen Victoria's Diamond Jubilee, is a splendid building paid for by Walter Morrison, a wealthy benefactor who lived at Malham nearby.

Morrison, Liberal Unionist MP for Skipton, was friends with Charles Darwin and Charles Kingsley who were entertained at his Malham estate; indeed, on a visit to Morrison's Yorkshire home, the latter was inspired to write The Water Babes.

In the early 1960s, as for decades, the chapel dominated the surrounding countryside and, as you approached Settle, the market town adjoining Giggleswick, its copper dome, turned turquoise by years of rain, lit up the Craven area, truly, a stunning sight.

Giggleswick celebrated its 500th anniversary in 2012, and while the status of the school suffered periodically in the 50s and 60s, recent headmasters have transformed its reputation and facilities.

Referring to headmasters reminds me of an amusing gaffe by my father in the late 1950s during a formal interview in the head's study which would help to determine my place.

Chatting informally before the serious business began, my father innocently asked the then head: "And how is one of your predecessors Mr Peacock?"

"I think you mean Mr Partridge."

Quick as a flash, my father replied: "Sorry I got the wrong bird".

My mother, wearing her best suit to impress the head, almost fell off the sofa in embarrassment.

My father's blunder did no harm to my chances of being offered a place, and looking back 60 years later, I still love my school, its high standards and the Giggleswick values, not least treating everyone with respect whatever their background.

The emphasis on sport I relished, playing in the same first X1 cricket team as Gordon Wilcock who later appeared regularly as a wicket-keeper for Worcestershire during the 1970s. Regarding rugby, second row forward Richard Trickey after he left Giggleswick in the 1960s became one of the best players not to be capped by England and is regarded as unfortunate not to have played at international level.

Among the many highlights of Trickey's career for Sale and Lancashire (100 caps when the County Championship was a major tournament) was playing a big role in the famous victory by the North West Counties against the All Blacks (16-14) at Workington in 1972.

Music and choral singing in the beauty of the chapel were permanent fixtures as was drama, but the quality of the plays produced was improved beyond recognition by Russell Harty, the Drama and English teacher, who went on to become a television star in the 1970s and 1980s on both ITV and the BBC.

At Giggleswick, Russell, youthful, witty, engaging and creative, came from a different generation to the other masters. He was more than a breath of fresh air. Harty's style in the classroom and on stage, made Shakespeare come alive.

Russell Harty – Chat show host in the 1970s and 1980s*

Macbeth and Hamlet were something to enjoy and not to be endured. Russell never seemed comfortable in sports gear on a cold and wet afternoon, but he sparkled putting together a series of plays which were fun for the participating boys whose confidence grew.

A close friend of Alan Bennett, a frequent visitor to Giggleswick in his grey flannels and sports jacket, Harty's legacy is lasting as the school's success in drama, which he did so much to forge, has grown and grown.

I had a good rapport with Russell. Complimenting me on my impersonation of a New York cab driver, he said I should consider acting as a career. Probably not, but a more helpful suggestion than that of the headmaster, Owen Rowe, who recommended to my parents I was cut out to sell second hand cars.

Giggleswick's budding chat show host eventually competed alongside Michael Parkinson on a rival channel interviewing celebrities from show business and in doing so achieved both high ratings and fame.

Russell's interviews with stars such as Danny Kaye, Rita Hayworth, John Gielgud and Ralph Richardson were popular and often acclaimed.

But one celeb's appearance is always remembered in discussions about his career as a TV personality himself: the interview with Grace Jones. A lady of many talents, model, singer, actress and song writer, Grace felt she was being ignored and consequently erupted and started slapping Russell.

Wrongly, it seems Russell is best remembered for this embarrassing outburst and incident on his show, he was far more accomplished; his professional impact was recognised in 1973 by being given the Pye Television Award for the Most Outstanding New Personality, and in 1980 Russell's standing as a top class entertainer was again reinforced by his fellow professionals by being chosen to be subject of This is Your Life, presented by Eamonn Andrews.

His end was less glamourous and much more painful. Sadly, Russell died at the age of only 53 in June 1988 from liver failure caused by hepatitis. Thankfully, he is not lost to Giggleswick because he's buried at St. Alkelda's church in the village.

Giggleswick School's delightful setting in the Craven area with its high fells, stone walls and limestone rock has nothing in common with the flashy, urban world of television, and yet not only did it produce Russell Harty, but Richard Whiteley too.

A close friend of Russell's, Richard, and I were in the same school House and years later we shared a desk in the Yorkshire Television newsroom. He was also cut down in his prime at only 61. He lost his life in June 2005 at Leeds General Infirmary from heart trouble and pneumonia. As with Russell's death, Richard's came as a big shock and, such was his popularity and skill as a presenter, his successors would be judged by his standards.

Richard Whiteley – Television presenter at Yorkshire TV 1968–2005 – Countdown presenter 1982–2005

Richard had several claims to fame: for more than 20 years he hosted Countdown and, indeed, was the first person to be seen on Channel 4 at 4.45pm on November 2nd 1982. The word game, then produced in Leeds at the studios of Yorkshire Television, launched the new channel.

Often wearing a garish jacket, Richard handled the contestants in a friendly and amusing way and even if his puns were laughed at, his easy style turned him into a national star; whereas before his recognition had arguably been restricted to the YTV region as the presenter of the company's evening news show, Calendar.

It was during an edition of Calendar in 1977 that Richard's popularity leapt and leapt. Bitten by a ferret which wouldn't let go of his finger for 30 seconds or so, the clip became one of the most favourite of television out-takes on programmes showing broadcasts that went wrong or were unintentionally funny.

Richard wasn't slow to see the humorous side of the item, and often quipped that when he died, the headline in the paper would be: Ferret man dies.

I probably got to know Richard better at YTV than at Giggleswick where he was five years my senior. His study was at the top of the corridor in Shute House. Mine was at the bottom, so our relationship was at a distance. Clever and unathletic, Richard loved Giggleswick, became a governor and in his will bequeathed a fortune to the school.

A television presenter's career can be short-lived, fame one minute, thrown into the dustbin the next. Richard, though, survived at the top for more than 30 years, not least because he was astute at quickly spotting any threat to his prime position.

I recall him asking me to find out about Richard Madeley who joined YTV from Border TV in Carlisle in the 1980s. Madeley cut a dash and was highly ambitious. His talent was not open to doubt, and it wasn't surprising that he left Yorkshire TV to join Granada in Manchester.

Whiteley, whose programme ratings were consistently high, saw off any danger, real or imagined, and because he had the backing of influential executives, remained one of the UK's best presenters until he was taken ill in May 2005.

Giggleswick School near Settle

Giggleswick School Chapel

CHAPTER FIVE

LIVERPOOL

As a late developer, who wasn't that sharp academically and, indeed, needed to re-sit my O Levels, I hadn't been expected to win a place at university, but surprising success at A Level in subjects that interested me, History, Economics, Politics and English, ensured I gained entry to Liverpool University to study Politics.

On reflection, it wasn't so much the university that I attended, although I did enjoy the course, it was the city which I identified with. I was thrilled to go to Liverpool which in 1967 still buzzed and throbbed with the excitement of the Beatles, Cilla Black and Gerry and The Pacemakers.

The atmosphere was optimistic and welcoming. The Scousers were warm, friendly and chatty, but above all else, sharply funny. You felt you wouldn't suffer loneliness in Liverpool. I loved the accent, and the city's papers, the Post and Echo, which covered football superbly, reflected the mass worship of Liverpool FC and Everton FC.

Many of my student friends also came from the North and, like me, felt at home in Liverpool. While Scousers can be instantly funny, their humour and approach may shock some people whose background is, shall we say, bookish and intellectual.

One of the female students on the Politics course, who achieved distinction in her social services career and later as an artist, came from the respectable suburbs of north London where nothing can prepare you for the crudeness she faced in the centre of a strange city. We had arranged to meet outside Lime Street station before going to the cinema nearby.

When we met, Averil was in floods of tears.

"What's the matter?"

"It's horrible. A woman has just told me to fuck off because I was standing on her fucking patch on the pavement."

It turned out that Averil, unknowingly, had trespassed onto the spot where a prostitute met her customers. She, the prostitute, must have thought that a competitor was muscling in. How wrong can you be.

On a much more pleasant note, the city landmarks were attractive, such as the Liver Buildings, the Walker Art Gallery, the Adelphi Hotel and the two impressive cathedrals, Anglican and Roman Catholic, close to the university. Liverpool because of its industrial and maritime heritage was a city of distinction and I was proud to be part of it.

As at Giggleswick, coincidentally at Liverpool University, I was to be influenced by someone who later, like Russell Harty and Richard Whiteley, went on to enjoy a glamorous career in television.

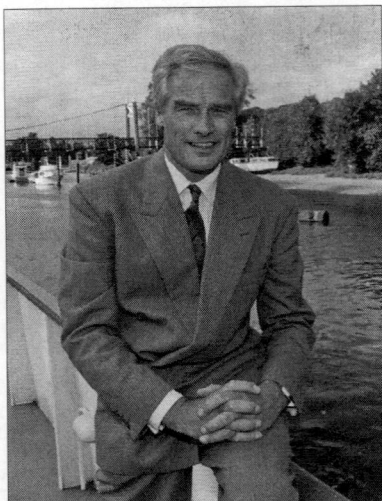

Robert Kilroy-Silk – Former Labour MP, MEP and TV presenter

Robert Kilroy-Silk lectured in Politics in a rather casual manner. His teaching style reminded me of the Irish comedian Dave Allen. Always smartly dressed, Kilroy-Silk possessed the look of a film star. Roger Moore comes to mind. I don't remember him lecturing from a lectern; his preferred method was to stand at the front of the lecture room and chat informally about Karl Marx. On occasions, Kilroy-Silk would sit on a stool and brush or flick his trousers just like Allen but without the humour.

A favourite with the female students, his chatty approach, later such a hit with studio audiences attending his BBC daytime show which ran for 17 years (1986-2004), meant Kilroy-Silk was a popular figure on the Politics course.

Before and after his television career, he put into practice, the political theory he taught. From 1974-83, Kilroy-Silk was the Labour MP for Ormskirk near Liverpool and between 1983 to 1986, he represented Knowsley North on Merseyside. His centre left views clashed with the rising power of Militant, the Hard Left group which was a force in Liverpool, and eventually Kilroy-Silk left Labour, scarred by the party's internal and bitter battles.

His experiences at the university were far less eventful and calmer, but subsequently controversy erupted. His show was cancelled by the BBC following remarks on Arabs. Meanwhile, Kilroy-Silk's political stance underwent a radical change as he was elected an MEP (Member of the European Parliament) for UKIP (the anti EU party) in 2004. But he also fell out with them and then set up his own party, Veritas, an unsuccessful move in which Kilroy-Silk suffered from further in-fighting.

In my student naivety, I had no idea of the deep and lasting personal bitterness which poisons British politics. I arranged speakers for the Politics Society at university and attracted a wide range of guests, including the left wing Labour MP for Liverpool Walton (1964-91), Eric Heffer. Chatting to him in the lift taking us to the Politics Department, I remarked that I admired Roy Jenkins, then Chancellor of the Exchequer in the Harold Wilson government. Jenkins, socially and politically, was poles apart from Heffer.

"That bugger enjoys taking afternoon tea with duchesses," was Heffer's caustic dismissal, emphasising his hostility to the social democratic strand in the Labour Party.

Heffer's talks on his constituency duties and on current issues, notably the Vietnam War, were more than matched by a similar visit by a truly national figure in Labour, Bessie Braddock, the MP for Liverpool Exchange from 1945-70.

A renowned fighter against poverty in Liverpool from her schooldays, this formidable lady, politically and physically, charmed us all. There was no hint of bitterness towards the privileged backgrounds many of my fellow students came from, unlike hers and her constituents, but instead Mrs Braddock delivered a passionate explanation of how she was tackling slum housing.

The talks by these two Liverpool MPs attracted little interest except from students studying Politics. However, and inevitably, an address by Enoch Powell, the controversial Conservative MP, not that long after his inflammatory Rivers of Blood speech at Birmingham in April 1968 against mass immigration, caused widespread opposition among students and some members of the university's staff.

Enoch Powell – Conservative MP 1950–1974 and Ulster Unionist MP 1974–1987

Before the noisy demonstration outside the Liverpool venue in the city centre his visit did not begin promisingly for me. On meeting Powell, who had been sacked from the Shadow Cabinet by Ted Heath, the Tory leader, at Lime Street station, I pointed out the waiting taxi.

Mr Powell opened the door and flung his black Homburg hat across the back seat. I didn't notice where his hat had landed because I was walking round to the other door to join him.

Embarrassingly, I sat on Enoch's headgear and crushed it. I apologised. He didn't say a word and proceeded to knock his hat back into shape. Within a minute or two, the ice was broken and the cab ride to the building where the meeting was being held was convivial.

The protests outside, although loud, were peaceful. The contents of Enoch's speech were unimportant, but what left a memorable impact was not what he said, but how Powell looked.

The UK's most divisive politician, strikingly pale I thought, gripped you with a cold, fixed stare that made you feel uncomfortable, but simultaneously held your attention.

On a less serious note, countless Saturday afternoons were spent at Anfield happily supporting Liverpool managed by Bill Shankly, loved by the red half of the city and I am sure respected by the blue half which shouted for Everton whose boss, Harry Catterick, was a less flamboyant character.

My first trip to Anfield is remembered not for the football but the incident didn't put me off. At half time on the Kop, a fan, unaware to me, peed on my navy blue donkey jacket. Later, I discovered the technique. He'd used a rolled up copy of the Liverpool Echo to control the urine or to increase its accuracy. Hence the expression a soggy Echo.

Much as I enjoyed standing on the Kop, the humour, the banners and the singing of You'll Never Walk Alone by Gerry Marsden and the Pacemakers, it was safer to transfer to the Paddock and watch from there as the touchline was just in front.

In my experience, the central point about Anfield is that you are trapped by the atmosphere and it never leaves you. As a student, the players of my era instantly became heroes, providing as they did thrilling entertainment on Saturdays and mid-week clashes when European matches were staged under floodlights that boosted the raw emotion in the ground.

The Paddock gave me a clear view to enjoy and applaud the skills of Peter Thompson who tortured defenders with his speed and electric ability to cross the ball.

Another favourite was also a winger, Ian Callghan, industrious and overflowing with energy. Cally never stopped running at his opponents, his cheeks bulging as he took them on.

In 10 years, Thompson appeared more than 400 times for Liverpool. Callaghan's fitness and durability ensured he was a permanent component, playing in an astonishing 857 games between 1960 and 1978; the highlight of his career came late as he won the European Cup in 1977 when Liverpool beat Borussia Monchengladbach by 3-1.

The players of the late 1960s gave so much pleasure and, in my case, other than watching the outstanding Wales rugby teams from same era and into the 1970s, I can't think of another group of sportsmen who produced such great entertainment which I saw regularly.

Peter Thompson

Manchester United fans will no doubt disagree. From the Paddock, the Kop was to the right, so you had a good view of Tommy Lawrence in goal, and the players in front of him. Gerry Byrne, Chris Lawler, Geoff Strong, Alec Lindsay, Ron Yeats, Willie Stevenson, Tommy Smith, Callaghan,

Thompson, Ian St John, Roger Hunt, Emlyn Hughes and Bobby Graham. They were joined later in my period at university by forwards Alan Evans and Tony Hately.

My favourite player, just behind Thompson and Callaghan, was striker Roger Hunt, a World Cup winner with England in 1966. Sport gives fans many memorable moments that are special to each individual; the sight of Hunt, turning away, arm aloft, after scoring in front of the Kop stands out to this day.

In all competitions, Hunt played 492 games, scoring 286 goals, a record until it was broken by Ian Rush, Liverpool's all time highest goal scorer with 346, spread across two spells, 1980-87 and then 1988-1996.

The fun and excitement on offer at Anfield lasted over the weekend and wiped out momentarily some of the dreary features of the Politics course. Marxist theory didn't produce many smiles.

In my era, Shankly sat in the directors' box behind the Paddock and close by was the press box where some reporters were phoning running copy to Saturday evening sports papers, such as the Pink 'Un and the Green 'Un, and others were composing their thoughts for Sunday's papers or Monday's.

Bill Shankly – Liverpool FC Manager 1959–1974

Liverpool has always been a good news area offering a rich variety of stories, other than football…dock disputes and strikes, crime, council tales, the courts and the cathedrals. The city's MPs, like Braddock and Heffer, were regular sources of strong copy. Locally and nationally, Liverpool born stars, notably The Beatles, and comedians Jimmy Tarbuck and Ken Dodd featured prominently.

So the area would have been the perfect place to learn the basics of journalism, but unfortunately my efforts to get a job on a paper in Liverpool failed, but several years later, I was able to meet professionally the city's biggest personality, Bill Shankly.

Winner of three Division One titles, two FA Cups, one UEFA Cup and three Charity Shields between 1959 and 1974, Shankly remained a colossus in retirement, retaining his charisma, Scottish growl, directness and humour.

Considering that he'd played successfully in the 1930s and after the Second World War for Preston North End (1933-49), Shankly was exactly the right interviewee to make a sparkling contribution to a documentary that Yorkshire Television broadcast on a famous footballer, Raich Carter who was a contemporary from the same era.

Raich Carter in his Hull City days with future Leeds United boss Don Revie.

Past Masters paid tribute to several distinguished sportsmen and women from the YTV area; in Carter's case he lived in Hull whose football team he'd played for and managed from 1948-52. He also played for England and Derby County, but initially Carter's fame was earned at Sunderland in the 1930s. A dazzling inside forward, Carter inspired them to win the First Division in 1936 and the year later he captained Sunderland to a 3-1 victory at Wembley in the FA Cup Final against Preston North End for whom Shankly was playing.

I wrote the script for the Raich Carter programme; my editorial duties also required me to research his career during a visit to his home at Willerby in Hull where he showed me a fine collection of carefully kept scrapbooks illustrating his glittering career at Sunderland, Derby County, Hull City and England.

Yorkshire Television also came across some cinema newsreel footage of the 1937 Cup Final showing action shots of Carter and Shankly.

"Of all my contemporaries, I'd love to see Bill again", he told me when YTV were setting up the programme.

Liverpool FC quickly supplied Shankly's home number which was answered by a familiar voice.

"I'd love to come over and you can tell Raich Carter I know more about him than he does himself. He was a great player and I've never forgotten Sunderland winning at Wembley. We'll have plenty to talk about. You don't need to organise me a taxi. I've got a taxi driver I've used for years."

Everything was put in place for the recording; however, embarrassingly it had to be cancelled. In the late 1970s, the unions were aggressive and powerful in commercial television and with ITV's management often willing to concede, the union officials knew they could demand more from an industry which was highly profitable.

The electricians on this occasion went on strike, so the Raich Carter programme could not be recorded which, therefore, meant that Shankly was making a wasted journey across the Pennines from Liverpool.

Nevertheless, he eventually arrived in reception at YTV looking pretty much the same as the figure I saw in the directors box at Anfield or being idolised as he celebrated another triumph, arms raised, in front of the Kop.

"Nice to meet you, son. Has Raich arrived yet?"

"No, Mr Shankly and I am afraid he won't be either."

"What do you mean? I've just come all the way from Liverpool."

"There's something I need to explain, Mr Shankly, because things have gone wrong."

"You seem a bit agitated son. We'd better go for a cup of tea."

Over tea in the YTV canteen, I explained about the strike and also explained that there wouldn't be one the following week, so we could then do the Carter programme as planned.

Shankly nodded and took it all in, and to my relief said he'd be happy to come back in a few days.

And then he shot out some words of advice before I introduced him to my bosses who were equally embarrassed that Shankly had made a wasted trip.

"Listen to me son. I've been around a lot longer than you and I can tell you this. There's always some bastard around who'll fuck you up.

"Now, let's finish our tea and then we can drive back."

As promised, he returned the next week and memorably lit up the studio with the Shankly wit, repartee and opinions on football since his retirement in 1974.

A lost soul without the drug of football, Bill Shankly died from a heart attack in late September 1981, aged 68.

Appropriately, his ashes were scattered at Anfield in front of the Kop.

Liverpool scenes, including the Roman Catholic cathedral and the Anglican cathedral.

CHAPTER SIX

ON THE AIR IN LEICESTER

The rough and tumble of Liverpool ended in the summer of 1970, and by September I had started my first job in journalism and broadcasting at BBC Radio Leicester, the first of the BBC's local radio stations which was opened in 1967.

Initially, I found Leicester, overall a prosperous city in the East Midlands, flat and featureless compared with the North East, Yorkshire and Liverpool. The people didn't appear to be as warm or friendly, and instead of calling you pet or luv, bus conductors, shop assistants or bar workers began a remark or ended it with, me duck.

However, within a few weeks, I settled in and grew fond of the city which gave a novice journalist plenty of opportunities. The training was on the job rather than the formal route taken by newspaper trainees, and the young reporters I met on stories had been better prepared than me.

Thrown in at the deep end did not mean I was not helped by the experienced journalists at the radio station or by the staff at the Leicester News Service, the agency which had a contract to supply news and sports stories, mainly on Leicester City, Leicester Tigers, one of the top rugby clubs in the UK, and Leicestershire County Cricket Club, then skippered by Ray Illingworth who was later appointed England captain.

Roland Orton, the owner of the news agency and a character well respected by the sports desks in Fleet Street, then the home of the UK's national papers, may have been a hard taskmaster, but his young reporters received a thorough training that opened up doors in the national press and broadcasting.

Some of the lessons rubbed off on me, and as a result of working closely with reporters at BBC Radio Leicester and at the Leicester News Service,

I learned the importance of clear writing, how to spot a news story, how to develop it, writing to length and how vital it was to write stories whose accuracy could not be challenged.

My job as a Station Assistant, the lowest rung on the BBC local radio ladder, combined technical duties with reporting. As well as covering stories and conducting interviews on a bulky Uher tape recorder, the tape which recorded the sound required editing and cut to the allocated length demanded by the News Editor.

Now all radio stories are edited digitally, then journalists used razor blades to slice the tape and remove parts of the interview that weren't needed.

The item on a plastic reel was now ready to be broadcast and put out over the airwaves via a large tape deck linked to the broadcasting engineering system in the studio and control room.

One of my main jobs was to make sure I pressed the right button in the transmission area so that the correct story was broadcast. Sometimes, I got it wrong, causing panic and embarrassment in the studio where the news presenters had to apologise immediately.

Local radio was hectic and fun, and to be given the opportunity to present the Saturday afternoon sports programme was quite special. I would write and broadcast introductions to live reports from wherever Leicester City were playing or where Leicester Tigers were fulfilling their latest first class fixture.

City, managed by the genial Irishman, Frank O'Farrell, won the Second Division title in 1970-71. Football was covered in great detail because of its popularity and editorially it was highly significant.

So stories on O'Farrell, whose success at Filbert Street, then City's home, persuaded Manchester United to appoint him as manager, were regular.

Similar coverage also applied to the big stars at Leicester City – goal-keeper Peter Shilton, capped a record 125 times by England, and strikers Frank Worthington, Rodney Fern and Alan Birchenall, an institution at the club, who once his playing career was finished returned to City as an ambassador and a pre-match and half-time host.

For more than 20 years, a familiar voice on Saturday afternoons was that of Van Hopkins, a Welshman who commentated on Leicester Tigers' games at Welford Road.

His deep voice rattled the stand as he described events; one particular player frequently mentioned in the powerful Tigers' pack was Garry Adey who made 381 appearances and was capped twice by England.

Flanker David Matthews, the greatest Tiger of them all in the judgement of many Leicester supporters, who played in 502 matches, was also a favourite of Hopkins.

The future England and British and Irish Lions hooker, Peter Wheeler, was establishing himself at the Tigers in my time. One of the club's outstanding forwards, Wheeler wore the Leicester jersey in almost 350 games between 1969 and 1985, playing an influential role as skipper of the sides which won in three consecutive years the John Player Cup at Twickenham in 1979, 80 and 81.

I used to enjoy his company over a couple of pints or so at the Bowling Green pub in the city centre on Friday nights. How things have changed since rugby union became a professional sport with its emphasis on players' fitness, the right diet and the dangers of alcohol.

In the decade ahead, Wheeler transferred his playing expertise to the boardroom at Welford Road. Appointed chief executive in 1996, he held top positions until retiring in 2015. By then, Wheeler had transformed the club commercially and the stadium too.

For a glorious period, the Tigers roared, winning the Premiership titles through the play-offs in 2007, 2009, 2010 and 2013. In between, Wheeler presided over success too in Europe as the Tigers dominated the Heineken Cup, winning it consecutively in 2001 and 2002.

So Van Hopkins, who retired as a commentator in the late 1980s, continued to enjoy the club's success from his seat in the stands until he died, aged 89, in 2014.

Interestingly, one of the players Van mentioned often in his match commentaries when I presented the sports programme, was fly half Bleddyn Jones, who succeeded him as BBC Radio Leicester's rugby broadcaster, a post he held for 30 years.

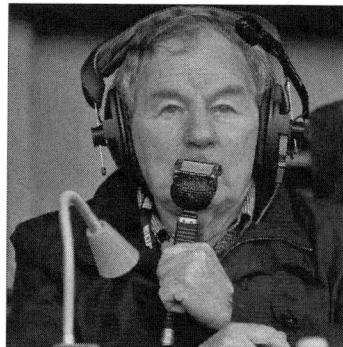

Bleddyn Jones

Chatting to him in the spring of 2020, Bleddyn (300 appearances for Leicester from 1969-78) brought back memories of an unpleasant conversation at the radio station in January 1970 within a few months of me joining the staff.

As a keen sportsman, I had been asked to look after and help technically two South African broadcasters who were in the UK covering the 1969-70 rugby tour by the Springboks. Several of the games had been the target of anti-apartheid demonstrators, including the game at Welford Road against Midland Counties East in November 1969.

The South Africans' second match in the New Year was at Coventry against Midland Counties West. The SABC (South African Broadcasting Corporation) had booked facilities at BBC Radio Leicester so that their two reporters, one covering for the English language service and the other broadcasting in Afrikaans, could file their reports.

Two hours after the game, the two South Africans arrived in reception where I was waiting to take them to the studio so they could broadcast their reports and interviews.

Unfortunately for them, the studio which had been booked was running late but not my much, so there was ample time for the deadline to be met.

The studio was being used by makers of the Asian programme that was broadcast weekly to the Asian population in Leicester; it's estimated that in the decade to 1978, more than 20,000 East African Asians, many of them kicked out of Uganda by the dictator Idi Amin, had settled in the city.

Understandably, as far back as 1970, the Asian community was significant and Radio Leicester played an important part in putting across information and news features to reflect that community's interests and concerns.

I apologised, but said the studio would be free in a few minutes. The South African whose first language was Afrikaans, spoken by the Afrikaners supporting the racist National Party governments in the apartheid era (1948-91), felt insulted.

"I'm not waiting around for any bloody kaffirs."

It was a horrible comment which I've never forgotten, and one remembered whenever I've done stories with South African cricketers and rugby players whose international careers were ruined by the isolation imposed by governments worldwide opposed to the suppression of the majority black and coloured population in the republic.

Grasping the chance to report on a wide range of news stories naturally put me in touch with Leicester's MPs who were keen to promote themselves and the interests of their constituents.

The first politician I had regular contact with, Greville Janner, a Labour MP in the city from 1970 until being made a Life Peer in the House of Lords in 1997, ultimately became a highly controversial figure. He was accused of child sex abuse which was vehemently denied by Lord Janner and his family.

In 2015, he was charged with sexually abusing nine alleged victims. Janner, in old age, suffered from dementia, and was unfit to plea. He died later that year before a trial of the facts could take place.

His son, Daniel, like his father a QC, said the allegations were rubbish, and in July 2019, Carl Beech was convicted of falsely accusing Janner and others of sexual abuse and murder. Beech was jailed for 18 years.

Greville Janner MP in the centre

Janner was well respected as a solid and hardworking MP on behalf of his constituents. My opinion was that he was pushy and ambitious and over keen on self-promotion as most politicians are.

What amused us most in the newsroom at Radio Leicester was that when Greville Janner had a story to promote he'd transfer the phone call from the House of Commons, so we ended up paying for it. We felt this was a bit much, but readily agreed to accept the charge when the operator asked us to because Janner often had a decent story.

Indeed, I had a lot to thank him for because on one of his regular visits to the newsroom on a Friday or Saturday morning, he gave me a story that proved to be a genuine thrill in my career.

Janner had been pressing Ministers for months to agree an attendance allowance for a teenager who was confined to a wheelchair; at last his efforts were successful and set a precedent so that others in similar stressful circumstances could also be paid.

This was a strong human interest story and one which attracted the attention of the Today programme, then, as now, the main current affairs show in the morning on BBC Radio Four.

My story, containing interviews with Janner and the teenage boy requiring the attendance allowance, was just over two and a half minutes in length, and when the introduction was read by presenter John Timpson, finishing with Guy Williams reports, it was quite something to hear your story on national radio at such an early stage in your career.

Trying hard to persuade producers on Today to take a strong regional story from you was the right attitude that many ambitious local radio reporters possessed.

The next opportunity came in 1972 as international opposition to apartheid in South Africa rose relentlessly and State oppression intensified in the republic against opponents of the National Party.

Surprisingly, one of the leading campaigners in SA against apartheid, Gonville Aubie ffrench-Beytagh, the Anglican Dean of Johannesburg, arrived unexpectedly in Ashy-de-la-Zouch, a quiet market town in Leicestershire, unused to being at the centre of a major news story.

The Dean fled South Africa in April 1972 after losing his appeal against his conviction and sentence under the Terrorism Act. He found sanctuary in Ashby which is where I met him. Articulate and charming and detailed in explaining how he'd been spied on by BOSS, the South African Bureau of State Security, Gonville Aubie ffrench-Beytagh put over brilliantly the case against apartheid and reinforced the arguments in favour of sanctions, both economic and sporting.

Selling the story to Today boosted my self-confidence and strengthened my conviction that I needed a proper training in journalism to support the practical experience I had gained in Leicester.

Amid the serious news coverage, lighter moments kept me amused. Being told to fuck off by George Brown, the former Labour Foreign Secretary in Harold Wilson's Labour Government, was a shock because it was late in the morning and I don't think that even George Brown had been drinking by then.

I always enjoyed carrying out street interviews, vox pops with passersby. Asked to seek a lady's opinion on the Budget, she replied: "I haven't a clue me duck. I've not fed it yet."

Pointing out that I'd not asked her about her budgie, but the budget, she asked: "What's he done for bird lovers?"

A feature on croquet with a very plummy county type in the Leicestershire countryside caused a lot of amusement in the newsroom. One of my duties was putting together features on minority sports, bowls, archery etc., and it was felt that croquet deserved a showing. The hunting areas of the county-titled families and landowners, had their fair share of eccentrics, so too croquet.

Having driven up a long tree lined drive, I knocked on the door of this lovely Regency house. The opening conversation was rather odd as I met the owner, dressed in a tasteful sports jacket and Cavalry Twills.

"Beer?"

"No thanks. My name is Guy Williams from BBC Radio Leicester."

"I'm sure you are, but I'm asking you if you want a drink."

"Perhaps we can have one once we've done the croquet interview."

"You'd better come into the drawing room."

We walked in briskly.

"Get out of the way while I speak to this reporter," my croquet contact barked at his Labradors.

"They are always in the effing way. Now, let me tell you about croquet. What you have to do is to swing your mallet between your legs and if I may say so without hitting your balls which would be rather painful."

"Having lined up your mallet, you then strike your ball. The object is to hit your ball through the hoop and hopefully knock the other chap's ball out of the way."

During this explanation, the labs had reappeared, interrupting this well informed discourse.

"I've told you before to get out of the way and there's always a chance that I may hit your balls with my mallet while I try to hit my ball through the bloody hoop.

"That's it really. It's all about getting your balls through the hoop."

John Cleese or Eric Idle could not have played the part more perfectly. The croquet story was broadcast and received warmly by the sport's or pastime's players. However, the producer of the sports programme did have reservations about putting it out, fearing the same people would feel we were taking the mickey.

Far from it. It was an accurate but amusing portrayal of croquet as explained by one of its keenest participants.

CHAPTER SEVEN

WORKING IN LONDON AND BEYOND

Such light hearted stories and humour quickly came to an end once I had completed the BBC's News Training Scheme, a prestigious opportunity which in 1972 accepted only 12 young journalists a year out of several hundred applicants.

Working, principally on the BBC Radio Four news desk, writing stories, was a serious business. Accuracy, above all else, was the guiding principle; and having had limited experience in provincial journalism, the chance to work in the London news room of the world's largest news organisation was an opening given to a few.

I particularly relished looking through the copy from international news agencies, such as Reuters or AFP (Agence France Presse), and the Press Association, supplying domestic news to the BBC, Independent Television News and national and provincial newspapers. You felt right at the centre

BBC HQ where I worked

of events, for example, the Vietnam War and the never ending crisis in the Middle East, and when the BBC's foreign correspondents filed their despatches from, say, Washington, Moscow or Jerusalem, the newsroom throbbed with excitement.

Many of the BBC's senior journalists running the news desks had previously been on Fleet Street's national papers, so someone as wet behind the ears as me stood out, but simultaneously you had every chance to learn if you had the talent and your face fitted.

I desperately wanted to be a reporter rather than a production journalist stuck inside behind a desk. I felt my character and personality were far better suited to being out and about, but when reporting jobs came up, however junior, I was rejected.

It was still, though, early days, but for a brief moment in March 1974, I foolishly thought I'd made a breakthrough and that my enthusiasm and hard work would advance my career.

Journalists need luck, and being in the right place at the right time and then delivering the story, often makes your career.

So the evening of Wednesday March 20th 1974 was, quite by accident, such an opportunity.

I'd arrived back in the newsroom and was one of only two sub-editors on the Radio Four news desk. A senior member of staff took a call from the Met Police advising the BBC that a serious incident had occurred in the Mall, but details were sketchy.

The editor in charge of the 10.00pm bulletin, Ken Goudie, a charming man who always seemed to wear red braces, calmly told me to jump in a taxi and get down to the Mall.

Once there, all I could see were police cars in the distance and flashing blue lights. I walked a few yards and instantly met a policeman.

"No further son. There's been a shooting and Princess Anne has been involved."

The attempted kidnap of the Queen's 24 year old daughter was sensational. As Princess Anne and her husband, Captain Mark Phillips, were returning down Pall Mall to Buckingham Palace from a charity event, the Royal limousine was forced to stop by a Ford Escort driven by Ian Ball. He jumped out and began shooting at the Royal car.

Princess Anne's personal bodyguard, Inspector James Beaton, reacted as he was trained to do, but his pistol jammed. Ball then shot him and also wounded the Royal chauffer. A constable who'd called for back-up was also shot.

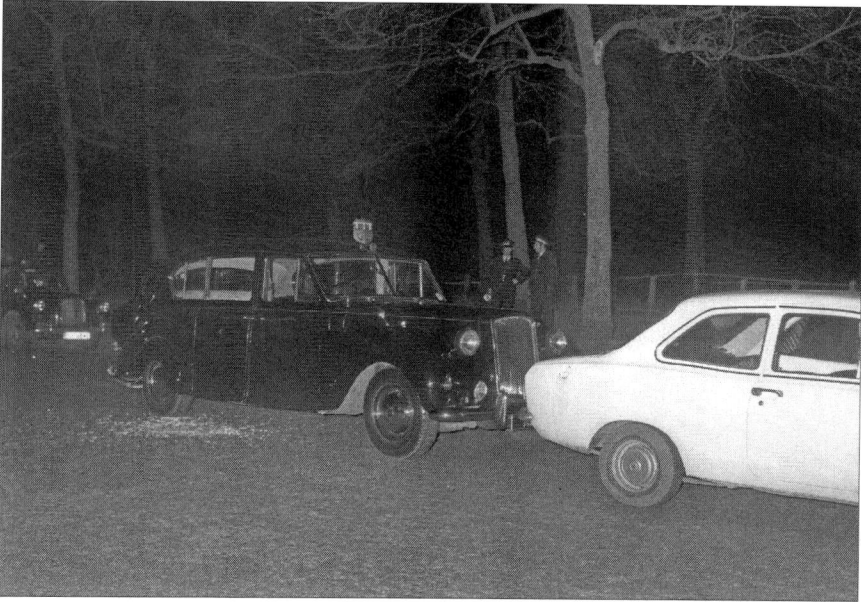

March 1974 – Kidnap attempt on Princess Anne

Ball was demanding a £2m ransom, coolly rejected by the princess who eventually, amid the drama and chaos, got out of the car and joined her lady-in-waiting.

A pedestrian who'd watched the crisis unfold intervened and hit Ball on the back of the head and led Anne to safety.

Meanwhile, a detective, who happened to be near the Mall, chased Ball and arrested him.

Later, during his court appearance, Ball pleaded guilty to attempted murder and kidnapping and was detained in Broadmoor under the Mental Health Act.

The events outlined were not immediately available when I arrived at the Mall, but I was able to put together a broad story that was strong enough to stress its scale.

Thankfully, the first door I knocked on opened and after convincing the home's owner that I was a BBC journalist who needed to use a phone straight away, I was able to tell the news desk in Broadcasting House the details of the biggest story I'd covered.

I was put through to the producer of the World Tonight, the current affairs programme which followed the 10.00pm Radio Four bulletin.

"Douglas Stewart, the presenter, will come to you in a minute or two and we want about 40 seconds to a minute on what you know."

Stewart had been a distinguished BBC foreign correspondent in the 1950s and 1960s, but was now presenting the World Tonight and conducting the programme's major interviews reflecting the day's important stories.

"There've been dramatic events this evening shortly before we came on air in Pall Mall where there's been an attempted kidnap of Princess Anne. Guy Williams has the details."

And off I went trying to report clearly what I knew about this huge story that could easily have resulted in the assassination of a member of the Royal Family.

Once my piece on the phone was over, I headed back to the newsroom, quietly pleased with my efforts, but knowing that far more experienced journalists would take over, and rightly so.

Nevertheless, rather like the satisfaction of producing stories for Today, I was thrilled to have done a live report into the World Tonight, a Radio Four outlet of equivalent status.

As a sub-editor, rewriting news agency copy into broadcast English where the sentences were shorter, the BBC were keen to use your skills outside the newsroom.

An enjoyable job for a period before I joined Yorkshire Television in September 1976 was spent in the Local Radio Parliamentary Unit in the House of Commons during Harold Wilson's second term as Labour Prime Minister from 1974-76.

My role involved some interviewing of MPs who'd raised constituency matters with Ministers, but in the main the BBC's local radio operation at Westminster centred on sending Press Association copy of importance to the stations up and down the country.

It satisfied my interest in politics, and being based at Westminster enabled me to renew my acquaintance with Sir James Kilfedder, a prominent Ulster Unionist MP and a future Speaker of the Northern Ireland Assembly from 1982-86.

Our paths first crossed in the late 1950s at Ramillies Hall School where this charming Irishman and barrister taught while I was a pupil.

I followed his political career off and on, but was naturally keen to meet him again now that 20 years later I was working in the House of Commons. At school, I'd remembered Kilfedder being attracted to the matron, and as inquisitive boys we would spy through the keyhole of the matron's bedroom to see what they were up to, not that we had much idea as 11 or 12 year olds.

At the same time as we thought Kilfedder was enjoying a passionate affair with the matron, it was also noticeable that he liked being in the company of boys, as you'd expect from a school teacher, but perhaps he was over familiar.

A most enjoyable dinner in the Members' dining room was arranged by Kilfedder at which we reminisced about our days at Ramillies Hall, but we also discussed the complexities of Ulster politics, the personalities involved and the Unionist perspective on the prevailing violence in the province during daily clashes between the British Army and the Provisional IRA.

Amusing and sharp in his observations, Kilfedder, MP for North Down (1970-1995) was charm personified, comfortably the type of politician a journalist would like to deal with whether his remarks were on or off the record.

Regularly reported in the media because of his significance in the affairs of Northern Ireland, Sir James died of a heart attack, aged 66, in March 1995. He died on the same day that the Belfast Telegraph put on its front page a story reporting that Sir James was one of several MPs contacted by the LGBT group, OutRage, asking them to come out as gay.

Looking back, Sir James was a serving MP in the late 1980s when I was asked to cover a left wing Socialist conference at Sheffield University at which one of the main speakers was Gerry Adams, President of Sinn Fein, the Irish nationalist party, and alleged to be a leading member of the Provisional IRA.

Given his background and unyielding Unionist convictions, you can imagine what Kilfedder's views would have been on one of his former pupils meeting an alleged IRA terrorist.

Gerry Adams President of Sinn Fein
1983–2018

During the Troubles in Northern Ireland in this period, television and radio companies were banned by law from broadcasting interviews with spokesmen of suspected terrorist organisations, such as the Provisional IRA.

We recorded the interview with Adams but afterwards his views had to be put out in reported speech over pictures relevant to the news item. So I took accurate notes of what Adams had said in the interview and in his speech and then broadcast them in my voiceover recorded at Yorkshire Television.

I remember feeling uncomfortable before interviewing Adams because I had shaken his hand, but there again it wasn't my role as an impartial journalist to make any judgement on the rights and wrongs of Ulster politics.

The story was strong enough to be used by ITN, ITV's national news company.

Before meeting Adams, Tony Benn, the former Labour Cabinet Minister but now leading the Left's opposition to the centrist policies of Labour leader, Neil Kinnock, had agreed enthusiastically to explain the purpose of the Socialist conference.

As the camera crew were setting up for the interview, Benn was keen to know whether they were trades union members and asked each in turn which union he belonged to.

As it happened, he didn't need to worry; both the cameraman and the sound recordist were fully signed up members of the ACTT, the Association of Cinematograph, Television and Allied Technicians, and the electrician had joined the Electrical, Electronic, Telecommunications and Plumbing Union.

Benn also politely asked me if I were an NUJ (National Union of Journalists) card holder.

On being reassured that we all understood and supported working class solidarity, Benn, once Viscount Stansgate, delivered a thought provoking interview; that made a change from an earlier attempt several years ago when Benn was Secretary of State for Industry in the Wilson Government.

"Not today, old boy," was his response as I approached him by the lift in the foyer of the department.

It was a surprising rejection because the BBC in Sheffield, where thousands worked in the steel industry, were convinced that Benn would take the opportunity to explain the Labour Government's attitude to the unions' requests for State aid.

Reporting in London for the BBC's local radio stations was not a full time role, so it was time to consider the next step in my career.

In Leicester, I'd met regional television reporters employed by the BBC in the Midlands and also journalists working for commercial television in Birmingham. My goal, therefore, was to try my luck in television and hope to achieve my ambition to become a regional TV reporter, either with the BBC or ITV.

My efforts succeeded because in the late summer of 1976, I was offered a job by Yorkshire Television in Leeds. The opportunity to return to the North on a similar salary to the BBC's in London made a lot of sense.

CHAPTER EIGHT

YORKSHIRE TELEVISION

My career at Yorkshire Television, one of the big players in the ITV system because of the quality of its programmes covering drama, light entertainment and documentaries, started perfectly.

My father insisted that I arrived early on my first day to show my keenness. The newsroom was deserted just after eight in the morning as I began reading the papers.

It surprised me, coming from the BBC where the newsroom operated 24 hours a day, that no one else was there. That, though, was about to change.

After about 15 minutes, I saw one of my boyhood heroes, surrounded by clouds of pipe smoke, walking up the corridor and into the newsroom.

Yorkshire Television building in Leeds

Ever since the 1950s and 1960s, I'd watched Fred Trueman bowling fast in Test matches on the BBC, broadcasting cricket in that era in black and white. His thrilling run-up to the wicket and classical side-on action produced a memorable spectacle.

Gloriously, the first bowler in the history of Test cricket to take 300 wickets, arguably Fred was now in the 1970s an even bigger personality than he had been in his first class career (1949-68) with Yorkshire and England.

Throughout the 50s and 60s, Fred's humour, bluntness and match winning spells had turned him into a top celebrity in the world of sport. More stories and controversies, true and false, were told about Fred Trueman than any other cricketer, and now several years into retirement from cricket, his fame still shone brightly.

He had established himself as a regular member of the Test Match Special team on BBC radio and at Yorkshire Television, he presented Indoor League, a pub game show with viewing figures of up to eight million.

Fred Trueman – Yorkshire and England fast bowler 1952–1965/67
Tests 307 wickets av: 21.57 ...1949–1969 603 matches 2304 wickets av: 18.29

Not only was I surprised to see Fred, but equally delighted when he strolled up to the news desk and introduced himself.

"Now then, I'm Fred Trueman."

"Yes, I know. Morning Mr Trueman. I've just joined Yorkshire Television and today's my first day."

"It's a good place to work. There's a good set of lads here and Uncle Fred will keep an eye on things. Do you like cricket then?

"I love it."

"Look, I've got to go now to record Indoor League, but I'll be in the bar downstairs at 12.30 and I'll see you there and introduce you to a few folk."

Gradually, in dribs and drabs, my new colleagues arrived, including my old school friend Richard Whiteley and Austin Mitchell, the main presenters of Calendar, YTV's evening news programme. Mitchell left television later and went into politics and served as the Labour MP for Grimsby from 1977 to 2015.

"Hello Richard. Guess whom I've just met?"

"Fred's a good bloke and if he says he'll be in the bar at lunchtime, he'll be there."

And he was. Fred introduced me to all sorts of people. Producers, reporters, cameramen, electricians, sound recordists and directors.

"I told you I'd turn up. Now, what would you like to drink?"

After a brief chat about Indoor League which was produced by Sid Waddell, the Geordie who enjoyed success as the Voice of Darts in the future, the talk naturally turned to cricket at my prompting.

"The best right handers I bowled to in my day were Peter May of Surrey and England and Everton Weekes, that fine West Indian. I don't think I ever saw the ball hit harder in my time than by Everton. May's on-drive was a fabulous shot and the sign of a really great player.

"And when it comes to left handers, there are two who stand out when I was playing. Neil Harvey of Australia and Garry Sobers from the West Indies, both were genuinely great batsmen."

"Isn't it time Fred, you were honoured? You've had nothing yet."

"Certainly is. Listen, sunshine, even Rachel Heyhoe fucking Flint has got the MBE. I've got nothing and all that charity work I've done."

And with that cutting and brutally funny remark, Fred said he was off.

Thankfully, there were several more occasions when our paths crossed professionally. Fred was always entertaining and informative, and his cricket brain and knowledge could hardly be bettered.

As regards Rachel Heyhoe Flint, then England's best known female cricketer and successful captain of the women's team (1966-78), she was awarded the MBE in 1972. Fred Trueman, described by Wisden Cricketers' Almanack, cricket's most authoritative book, as "probably the greatest fast bowler England has produced", received an OBE in 1989.

My first six weeks at Yorkshire Television were spent boarding at a guest house on Cardigan Road in Leeds, close to the Headingley cricket ground, and a stone's throw from the company's studios on Kirkstall Road.

Vi, who ran the bed and breakfast in what had been a smart Victorian or Edwardian house, was given a lot of business by YTV. Visiting actors, producers and directors were put up there, so it was rather like a theatrical digs, but the entertainment came free of charge.

The comic genius of Leonard Rossiter, star of YTV's Rising Damp who played Mr Rigsby, was a fellow guest.

Leonard Rossiter star of Yorkshire Television's Rising Damp 1974–78

Breakfast in the morning was hilarious, almost as funny as the sitcom (1974-78) in which Rossiter performed alongside Richard Beckinsale, Don Warrington and Frances de la Tour.

Margaret, the breakfast waitress and a bit long in the tooth, had, thankfully, a good sense of humour because she didn't know whether she was coming or going as a result of Rossiter's antics.

"What would you like this morning, Mr Rossiter?"

"I'm going to have the kippers."

With that, the kippers were ordered from the kitchen.

Seconds later: "I'm sorry Margaret. I've changed my mind. I'll have the beacon and eggs."

As the kitchen was close to the dining room, Rossiter's instructions could be heard clearly.

"Alright, Mr Rossiter."

Seconds later: "Margaret, I've changed my mind again. I'll have the scrambled eggs."

And so the fun and games continued until Margaret, pretending to be cross, came back into the dining room.

"Do you know, Mr Rossiter, you're a right one you are."

Margaret was a good judge.

Rising Damp was one of the most popular sitcoms in the history of British television, and produced by a company which won many awards for the high standards of its wide ranging output.

Since YTV opened in 1967, it had attracted the best talent and many household names in the industry.

In comedy, drama and light entertainment, for example, Les Dawson (Dawson's Weekly), Rik Mayall(New Statesman), Molly Sugden in That's My Boy and Jimmy Tarbuck presenting Winner Takes All.

David Jason starred in a Touch of Frost, Darling Buds of May and A Bit of a Do. Emmerdale Farm, later changing to Emmerdale, was hugely popular and Heartbeat was another national hit.

Just as commercially successful were science and documentary programmes, such as Arthur C. Clarke's Mysterious World and Four Hours in My Lai, an investigation into a massacre by US soldiers during the Vietnam War.

First Tuesday, presented by Jonathan Dimbleby and Olivia O'Leary, similarly built a first class reputation.

The mega stars, though, were by a large margin David Frost and Alan Whicker, both television greats over many years.

Frost presented Through the Keyhole where a panel of celebrities had to guess the name of another celebrity whose house and contents were on display to the viewers.

On a more serious note, YTV and Frost produced and presented a prestigious programme, A Prime Minister on Prime Ministers, in which the former Labour PM, Harold Wilson, returning to his West Riding roots, analysed the former occupants of 10, Downing Street.

Whicker's World, put together in Leeds between 1968 and 1983, won many awards as did its famous presenter and reporter. Alan Whicker travelled the globe tackling a vast array of topics, interviewing people right at the centre of his stories, and not only the rich and glamorous.

One particular success was his programme. Papa Doc, The Black Sheep. Whicker's documentary on the Haitian dictator, Papa Doc Duvalier.

So, that's a glimpse of my new employer; the first day had been remarkable because of the unexpected chat with Fred Trueman, but at the end of the week, for a few minutes I seriously thought I'd be shown the door.

Monday to Friday had been spent writing stories for Calendar News which was broadcast at lunchtime and then for 30 minutes early in the evening. On the Friday morning, shortly after my colleagues on the newsdesk had arrived for work, they began filling in green forms to claim expenses.

Being wet behind the ears, if not sodden, I asked how they could claim anything when they'd not left the building for five days.

"You can claim for a few quid for travelling. Just say you've covered a mill fire in Cleckheaton and you'll be fine," was the advice.

So I filled in my expenses form: Leeds-Cleckheaton-Leeds, 25 miles. Interview West Yorkshire Fire Chief, Mill Blaze.

I forget the amount claimed, but it wasn't much and didn't feel the claim would be questioned.

Half an hour after the editorial meeting to decide what would be in that night's Calendar, my boss, having seen the claim in his in-tray, wandered over.

"Guy, can I have a word about your expenses? Come into the office. Shut the door and remember this conversation did not take place."

"Listen, I'm really sorry. I know I've not been anywhere and it won't happen again. I apologise again."

"Guy, it's OK. Don't worry. Go away and do your expenses again. They are too low. Come back and I'll sign them."

Somewhat surprised, if not relieved to be still in a job, I filled in another form; this time I added on coverage of a pile-up on the M62, and a story with a council leader.

The expenses were re-submitted and approved. This free flow of cash continued for six weeks, my training period in Leeds.

Entertaining the leader of the council in Dewsbury became a regular event and I'm sure he enjoyed his fictitious weekly lunch as much as I did.

My claims were by no means as imaginative as a colleague's. Claiming to be hard up one Christmas, he rang up his butcher and asked how much the meat bill would be.

Writing down what was owed for the Christmas turkey and ham etc, the sum was quickly converted into mileage, and soon afterwards, the green form had been signed and the money collected from the cashier's office.

If you think that claim was creative, 10 years later when I was covering cricket for The Sunday Times, laughter erupted in the press box at Headingley when an experienced national newspaperman proudly announced that he'd be claiming reverse mileage, backing his car out of the garage at home. He'd done the sums and they added up to a tidy amount.

CHAPTER NINE

THE HUMBER LIFEBOAT AND THE DEATH OF HULL'S FISHING INDUSTRY

My mileage to Hull after training in Leeds was perfectly legitimate. I was hired as the Hull reporter and was glad to be returning to the city where I had enjoyed a period as a trainee journalist in the early 1970s at BBC Radio Humberside.

My job was to provide daily news stories from East Yorkshire, York and parts of North Yorkshire, including Scarborough. The region was large and varied; industrial, rural and possessing a beautiful coastline which attracted thousands of visitors, enjoying the charm of Filey, Flamborough Head and the harbour and beach at Bridlington.

Certainly, a splendid coast, but deadly too as generations of seafarers had lost their lives in the stormy waters of the North Sea. Arguably, the most eye catching feature of the Yorkshire coast in the Hull area was and is a thin strip of land, three miles long, stretching out to sea from the mainland.

At the estuary of the river Humber and home to a nature reserve run by the Yorkshire Wildlife Trust, the end of this tidal area is known as Spurn Point which can be one of the coldest and most uncomfortable places in the country.

Distinctively, it's the headquarters of the Humber lifeboat, manned by the only full time professional crew in the UK.

Risking their lives to save the lives of others in deep distress, the RNLI (Royal National Lifeboat Institution) crew are the bravest of the brave, none more so than Brian Bevan, the heroic coxswain who is credited with saving the lives of at least 300 people during his 35 years of gallant service, 26 as coxswain, before his retirement in 2001.

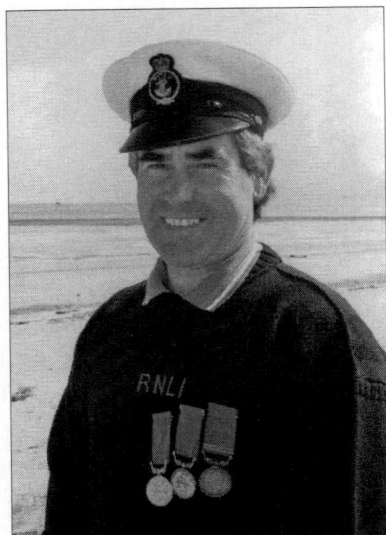

Brian Bevan
Coxswain of the Humber Lifeboat

Those of us who live safe lives where danger seldom threatens will find it difficult to understand the frightening challenges Bevan and his successors faced and face.

Totally selfless, Bevan was a modest man with nothing to be modest about; and given the stress and strain he endured during rescues in mountainous seas, it said a lot about his character that he was always willing to talk to inquisitive reporters such as myself on returning to Spurn Point.

In a calm, matter of fact way, as if he was pushing a trolley in Sainsbury's, Brian would explain how a dramatic rescue unfolded and how he and his crew took it in their stride.

His courage and leadership skills, recognised by the Queen with the award of the MBE in 1999, were severely tested in seven remarkable weeks only a few years after being appointed coxswain in 1975.

In late December 1978, Brian and the Humber lifeboat rescued six people, including a 12 year old girl, from a Dutch ship in an operation lasting 13 hours at sea. He was presented with a Silver medal by the RNLI.

A Gold medal swiftly followed after Brian excelled himself on Valentine's Day in February 1979. The Panamanian freighter, Revi, was sinking off Spurn Point. In waves of more than 30 feet high, four crew members were rescued after several attempts by the City of Bradford IV, the lifeboat.

At one point, the boat's crew came close to death as did the Revi's skipper who was clinging to the ship's rails. Eventually, he and his ship's crew jumped on to the lifeboat and were saved. Minutes later, the ship rolled over and disappeared.

Twenty four hours later after arriving back safely, Bevan was back at sea; this time to help the Romanian ship, Savinesti, with 28 on board. This operation was to last 17 exhausting hours.

The vessel, 37 miles off Spurn, was in danger of running aground because of engine failure. She'd lost both her anchors too. In a hurricane and in poor visibility because of thick snow, and with ice covering the lifeboat, Bevan escorted the Savinesti to the river Humber in sub-zero temperatures and rough seas.

As a result of his courage and that of his crew in these three rescues, Bevan became the only person in the history of the RNLI to be presented with a Gold, Silver and Bronze medal for gallantry at the same awards ceremony.

Inevitably, Yorkshire Television and the BBC in Leeds publicised these feats, but Brian's fame was beginning to spread and, therefore, his achievements caught the imagination of national television and the producers of This is Your Life, presented by Eamonn Andrews.

So in March 1980, Brian Bevan, at the age of only 24, was shocked to meet the smiling Irishman handing over the Big Red Book containing his life story.

The programme, produced by Thames Television, watched by millions, was broadcast a few weeks later.

Journalists because of their job are fortunate to meet and interview a wide range of people from all backgrounds, whether they are film stars or fire fighters, dukes or dustmen. In my experience, I've never met a braver man than Brian Bevan or one whose courage in terrifying conditions was repeated so often.

Just as Spurn Point has unusual characteristics, so does Hull and these are noticeable when you drive into the city.

Cream phone boxes instead of red make Hull unique, but no one seems to know precisely why the colour is different to the rest of the UK.

The reason why Hull adopted cream probably had much to do with the local authority, and not the Post

Hull's traditional cream phone box

Office, operating telephones in the city once it was granted a licence in 1902.

Hull City Council ran the telephones until their phone company was privatised in the late 1990s. Hull remains the only city with its own independent phone network managed now by KCOM, formerly KC and Kingston Communications.

As well as cream phone boxes, Hull has an accent that's nothing like the rest of Yorkshire.

Some people tried to hide it, but not always successfully. The receptionist at the Yorkshire Television office in Hull, an elegantly dressed lady called Barbara, spoke 99 per cent of the time without an accent, but on one occasion her true roots reappeared.

In tones that would not have been out of place at Buckingham Palace, she rang my office upstairs to tell me:

"Guy, I'm buzzing you online wun."

"Who is it Barbara because I'm a bit busy?"

In the rush to get rid of the caller and hand him over to me, she replied:

"I dern't nurh, but I think he's from Rurhvers."

Hull Kingston Rovers were and are one of two professional rugby league clubs in the city; the other being Hull F.C.

Barbara's slip of the tongue was not only amusing, but a reminder that Hull stands out. Suggestions that it was isolated from the rest of Yorkshire were, in my opinion, always exaggerated, but Hull is proud of its independence and of the rapid strides it has made (City of Culture in 2017) to improve the economy and attractions following the collapse of the fishing industry.

For example, The Deep, a huge aquarium, Hull Marina and Prince's Quay Shopping Centre, built at Prince's Dock, have helped to transform the port.

In the 1970s, regional television news coverage from Hull was dominated by the sad decline of fishing. Cod Wars were fought with Iceland who imposed a 200 mile limit in 1976 as did other countries where Hull's distant water trawlers worked. Joining the EU added to the misery and with the industry lacking the political clout of the miners, successive British governments presided over the collapse. Therefore, Hull's trawlers had nowhere to fish.

The Deep – a major Hull attraction

Like the lifeboatmen at Spurn Point, the city's fishermen were a special breed, earning a living in treacherous seas around Iceland, Russia and Norway.

Fishing in Arctic waters on trips lasting 20 days was hard and dangerous. Shifts of 20 hours were not uncommon. It's estimated that 6,000 Hull trawler men died at sea between 1835 to 1980.

One of the worst losses of lives occurred in 1968 when the city was devastated by the deaths of more than 50 fishermen in less than a month between January and February as three trawlers, St Romanus, Kingston Peridot and Ross Cleveland sank.

In the late 1970s to 1981 during my period as the YTV reporter, the prosperity of the 1950s was disappearing quickly. Thirty years previously, the Hull fish docks were overflowing with trawlers; more than 300 employing 8,000 men, and away from the fish quay, three times that figure earned a living from fish processing.

During a debate in the House of Commons, the Labour MP, James Johnson, who represented Hull West where many fishermen lived, described the plight of the industry in February 1979.

"I came to Hull 20 years ago and we had 130 boats in the dock and 600 men to unload them. Five years ago, two thousand fishermen were on the dock. Today, it's just over 1,000."

Hull's fish docks at their peak

Kits of fish ready for auction

Doing stories with trawler owners, skippers, deck hands and fish merchants was rewarding because they were eager to discuss issues and influence public opinion, but simultaneously the crisis made you feel uncomfortable because you were watching the death of what had been one of the world's major fishing ports.

The result was the hardship to families living in and around Hessle Road, home to many fishermen and close to the fish docks.

In 1970, Hull landed 197,000 tonnes of fish; by 1981, this figure had slumped to only 15,000 tonnes.

A way of life was drawing to a close. A new fish market was shut in 2011, and although 700 tonnes was unloaded in September 2018, the first time a trawler had landed fish for at least a decade, a once thriving industry had been reduced to a museum exhibit.

Perhaps the most interesting way of understanding the fishing industry in Hull is to visit the Maritime Museum in Queen Victoria Square. In addition to seeing whaling and trawling displays, you get a thorough education into how tough the life was of a trawlerman. Listen to the recorded interviews, and you'll instantly appreciate why the sea can be so cruel.

CHAPTER TEN

FROM HULL, GUY WILLIAMS REPORTS

I was to live and work in Hull happily for more than three years, and on reflection given the city's maritime heritage, it was appropriate that on my first working day as a reporter, I was thrown journalistically into the deep end.

The phone call I took from the press office at Humberside Police was rather understated.

"There's a bit of trouble at the prison. You should get yourself there."

As events proved, it was much, much more than a spot of bother. Overnight, a full scale riot at Hull jail, opened in 1870, on Hedon Road had exploded as more than 100 prisoners went on the rampage smashing everything in sight.

In three days of rioting, two thirds of the jail was destroyed in a protest against alleged brutality by prison officers. The rioters, several on the jail's roof throwing tiles at warders and other staff below, were in control having initially survived pitched battles against officers armed with riot shields and clubs.

The rioting was the worst trouble at a British prison since the mutiny at Dartmoor in 1932. In order to regain control, dozens of reinforcements were sent in from jails in Leeds and Wakefield.

Until the Home Office, then the Whitehall department responsible for prisons, gave permission for Yorkshire Television to film inside, the extent of the damage could not be clearly understood from the outside. On arrival, the cameramen I was working with were able to take shots of the rioters on the roof and, indeed, the sound recordist could also pick up their shouts.

Interviews were quickly done with eyewitnesses, senior police officers and representatives of the Prison Officers' Association, in time for YTV's

Hull prison riot and damage

lunchtime news. Their accounts were first rate and used on the ITN lunchtime bulletin too. Later on Day One of the riot, ITN asked me to put together a report for their early evening news programme. Naturally, as the size of the story unfolded, ITN sent their own reporter to cover what was for three days a big national event.

Soon after a negotiated settlement with the rioting prisoners had been agreed, the Home Office allowed reporters inside the jail. Wreckage was spread everywhere. Two of the of wings had been ripped to pieces. Furniture in cells had been smashed and piled high to make barricades against advancing prison warders. One memory that stands out is the mountain of white broken urinals and sinks which had been torn away with great ferocity from the walls.

Violence and hatred of the regime which ran Hull prison produced images for television news and newspapers which the public had not seen for many years. It was quiet an eye opener. The riot's damage was so vast that the jail was closed for a year while repairs costing almost £4m were carried out. More than 200 inmates had to be transferred to other jails.

A few years later, I returned to the prison on another story involving a visit by Douglas Hurd, the Home Secretary between 1985-89 during Margaret Thatcher's third term as Prime Minister. Hurd, a prison reformer and not on the same wavelength as the hangers and floggers in the Conservative Party, was inspecting a youth offenders' wing.

As the media and Hurd were being shown around, the stench was sickening because the walls had been smeared with excrement. Embarrassingly, I was sick on the spot; thankfully, the Home Secretary didn't notice and once outside in the fresh air I felt better and able to interview him about Home Office prison policy.

Regional television news was always keen for reporters to look out for lighter stories because bulletins were rightly dominated by serious stories such as serious crime and strikes. So if you came up with a tale that was amusing and one which viewers would enjoy, the chances of it being broadcast were high.

One such story came from Goole, a busy inland port roughly half way between Hull and Leeds and just off the M62.

A pet shop owner kept a parrot which had been taught to swear, but it wasn't mild swearing that you might have got away with if the odd bloody had been broadcast.

However, this parrot's language was shocking and as soon as you walked through the front door, a torrent of foul four letter words flew out.

"Look at this t—t who's come in."

Now many people, some well-known have sworn at me, probably with justification, but this was the first time I'd been insulted by a parrot.

To begin with, it was amusing, but it was soon realised that the bird's clearly enunciated words made them unfit to be heard on an evening news programme watched by families and children.

Still, the story was filmed; four letter words as well as clean passages when the pet shop owner persuaded his parrot to behave.

We had a silly story in the can which turned into an even funnier item once the sound specialists and picture editors in Leeds added many bleeps to kill all the four letter words.

Viewers at home saw the close-up shots of the parrot in his cage followed by a sequence of bleeps, lasting about a minute, over his swearing. The newsroom was in stitches. The funny but filthy parrot was a strong example of Yorkshire Television's approach to news; naturally, serious stories which affected viewers' lives were explained in depth, but the main presenters of Calendar, Richard Whiteley and Austin Mitchell, he in particular, were encouraged to act the fool where necessary so the audience could have a good laugh.

There must be something about the Goole area that naturally leads to comic moments, whether intended or not.

A story in Snaith caused a lot of hilarity and was thought to be so daft that all of 13 seconds were used on ITV's, It'll Be Alright on the Night, presented by Denis Norden, the comedy writer.

The programme specialised in hilarious blunders that occurred in the shooting of films and television shows, including news.

I was certainly not looking for national fame, however brief, when setting off for Snaith to chat to a retired railwayman who'd built a model steam engine and track in his garden.

The problem was the weather. Filming conditions were not easy because of rain and a strong wind, both of which made it difficult to see the rail enthusiast.

Unfortunately, clouds and clouds of smoke from the model steam loco continually blew into our faces and across the camera lens as we filmed our ride.

Every so often, I could be seen as the thick smoke cleared, but then I'd disappear as would the driver. A proper conversation or interview was not possible, but I persisted through the smoke and coughs, and when the loco ground to a halt I thought the story would be well received in Leeds.

Not so. One of the editors screamed down the phone and told me it was one of the worst pieces of television reporting he'd ever seen and it was almost impossible to cut, and to make things worse: "I want to see you tomorrow."

The story was broadcast the same day and looked perfectly acceptable, so much so that when I walked into reception at YTV's studios in Leeds the following afternoon, the commissionaire said he'd taken several phone calls from viewers saying how much they'd enjoyed watching the steam loco piece.

Colleagues in the newsroom also thought it'd been funny and, much to my relief, the expected bollocking didn't take place, so I still had a job.

But the best was still to come. I'm still not sure why I got a fee from It'll be Alright on the Night because YTV held the copywright. Nevertheless, the cash came in handy as did the $200 received from Dick Clark Productions in Hollywood who rang my home asking permission to use the 13 seconds which had been used on network television over Christmas in the late 1970s.

Obviously, it was fun to see Norden introduce the clip on his show, but I didn't see the US version go out.

The Snaith steam loco story and all the smoke wiping me and the engine out knew no bounds. Amazingly, Ugandan TV saw fit to show it. I'm not sure how much they paid, but only a few pounds, and the humour appealed to a television producer in Iceland too.

I've seen it said that some people achieve 15 minutes of fame. I managed only 13 seconds, but at least I can say, and not many UK reporters can, that I appeared on television in both Uganda and Iceland.

My editorial area because it stretched up to the coast to Bridlington and Scarborough supplied similar comic moments which appeared on YTV's evening news.

The holiday towns had venues large enough to put on shows featuring many of the biggest stars in show business. The singer and drag artist Danny La Rue, lit up in sequins, entertained me royally in his dressing room in Scarborough, readily agreeing to interrupt a rehearsal for his evening show.

Les Dawson

Comedian Freddie Starr, appearing in Bridlington, grasped at the opportunity to take the mickey out of Richard Whiteley in a priceless routine during which the cameraman struggled to shoot the item because he was laughing so much.

Bridlington, too, was the setting for a truly daft sketch that Les Dawson – has there ever been a funnier British comedian? – brilliantly performed on the beach in the pouring rain.

With each of us wearing a mack and sou'wester, and sitting in deck chairs, Les's one liners about how superior Bridlington was to Scarborough in every conceivable way, even its rain was less wet, were rapid ad-libs of a genius.

On and on he joked. You didn't notice, he said, Bridlington's cold winds when you came but Scarborough's were freezing, and as for the fish and chips, come to Brid every time, advised Les.

The item finished with both of us struggling to get out of the deck chairs which had sunk in the sand, and the pair of us making a mess of folding them up.

Les Dawson's willingness in Bridlington to cooperate with a YTV news reporter and to deliver instantly so many gags was remembered fondly by Calendar as YTV paid their respects to the comedian soon after he died in Manchester in June 1993.

In addition to showing clips from Les's YTV shows, Dawson's Weekly and Sez Les, in which he starred with Roy Barraclough as Cissie and Ada, Calendar played again some of the footage shot in the late 1970s on the beach at Brid.

It's fair to say that the more I worked in Hull, the more I realised that people in other parts of Yorkshire had little idea of how impressive a city it was and is.

As with Liverpool, the public buildings are most attractive, and following the success of the City of Culture in 2017, Hull's status has grown and grown.

The city centre contains numerous sights which stand out; among them, the Guildhall, Ferens Art Gallery and the monument to William Wilberforce, the Hull born MP who led the campaign to abolish the slave trade resulting in the 1833 Act of Parliament.

There are, though, other notable features including Hull Minster, previously known as Holy Trinity, the largest parish church in England, Queen's Gardens and Wilberforce House, the home of William who represented Hull in the 18th century (1780-84) and later Yorkshire in Parliament from 1784 to 1812.

A wander through the Old Town takes you to a narrow street called the Land of Green Ginger which apart from being a regular pub quiz question (where is it?) is where you can see what's considered to be the world's smallest window, just a slit through which the gate keeper at the George Hotel looked as stage coaches and passengers arrived.

In the same historic district, you'll find in Silver Street the best known pub in Hull, Ye Olde White Harte, built in 1550.

Ye Olde White Harte Pub

Oak panelled walls and inglenook fire places create an atmosphere reinforcing the view that history oozes throughout. Indeed, it's speculated

The skull in pub's case

that Ye Olde White Harte was the setting for a defining moment in the affairs of this country; in an upstairs room the decision was taken by the governor of Hull, Sir John Hotham, to prevent King Charles the First in April 1642 entering the city at Beverley Gate, one of four medieval entrances. Hotham's act of rebellion, designed to stop the king seizing a big stockpile of weapons, sparked the English Civil War between Charles and Parliament.

As you enjoy your drink in the pub, you may also be tempted to look at the skull encased behind the saloon bar. No one is quite certain what the origins are of this bizarre relic. Is it the scull of a youth who was smashed on the head by a drunken sea captain wielding a pistol, or can it be the remains of a serving girl whose body was hidden in the pub's attic after she'd been killed by the landlord?

Whatever the truth, the scull was discovered after a fire at Ye Olde White Harte in the 19th century.

Naturally, Hull is proud of its past, but the emphasis now since the death of the fishing industry is to accelerate the regeneration which has gone ahead. One of the best examples of the revival is The Deep, opened in 2002.

This spectacular aquarium contains more than 3,500 fish, including sharks. Over eight million visitors have seen the marine life on display in a facility which has established a top class reputation.

Talking of facilities in the Hull area to improve its economy, one of the major stories covered regularly was the building of the Humber Bridge, opened in 1981. As you drive across the M62 from Leeds and then on to the A63 towards Hull, the sight of the country's largest single span suspension bridge is quite stunning.

The roadway, stretching almost a mile and a half, connects the north bank at Hessle near Hull to the south bank at Barton-upon-Humber in North Lincolnshire.

Humber Bridge

Each massive tower is 510 feet tall. The economic benefits of the bridge have been significant; for instance, the journey from Hull to Grimsby was cut from 82 miles to 42. This landmark had more than its fair share of controversies, both political and financial, and during the bridge's construction, labour relations were at times tempestuous. From a television reporter's point of view, its gradual building and the location produced impressive pictures which made an impact on the screen.

As the bridge was being built, I was offered the opportunity to go across on the narrow catwalk from the Hull side to the other. Progress was slow as you took one careful step at a time. The presence of the safety net below did not remove the fear I had, particularly when told that no one would survive the dangerous torrents and freezing waters of the Humber if you fell in.

John Prescott Deputy Prime Minister 1997–2007 and Labour MP for Kingston upon Hull East 1970–2010.*

During this period in the late 1970s, the importance of being surefooted was recognised as an essential quality in politics by John Prescott, the Labour MP for East Hull who was then building his career.

Who would ever imagined that Prescott would become such an influential figure in British politics, rising to Deputy Prime Minister under Tony Blair from 1997 to 2007?

This is not the place to repeat the importance of Prescott in Labour or national politics; nor is it an opportunity to revive the scrapes and sex scandal which engulfed the former Deputy Leader of the Labour Party.

First elected as MP in 1970, Prescott, an ex-left wing official of the National Union of Seamen, represented Hull East in Parliament for 40 years until he was appointed a Life Peer in 2010.

*   *By Andrew Skudder - https://www.flickr.com/photos/skuds/4174928971/, CC BY-SA 2.0, https://commons.wikimedia.org/w/index.php?curid=67725661*

As a reporter, he was fun to deal with; and as Prescott readily understood he could use regional television to benefit himself and his constituents. You were, therefore, never short of stories.

Popular and well respected in Hull and beyond, especially in the trade union movement, I was surprised on one occasion why Prescott should be so cautious before I did an interview in his garden.

It was no secret that he lived in a Tudor style house which was built in 1906 and had eight bedrooms.

In a safe Labour seat, would it matter if voters saw the size of his home?

Nevertheless, Prescott insisted that the camera shot and where he stood for the interview should avoid giving the impression that their MP lived in great style.

"I don't want them to think I'm living in a mansion," he said.

John Prescott need not have worried. A fighter by nature and a political warrior involved in countless internal Labour battles, he fought and won 10 parliamentary elections in Hull East and attending his count on election night was always entertaining because of the banter he had with the media.

The future Deputy Prime Minister took advantage of what the city had to offer; one achievement Prescott is most proud of was graduating from Hull University in 1968 with a degree in Economics and Economic History.

Considering his long association and affection for the city, when he retired from the House of Commons and given a peerage so that he could sit in the House of Lords, not surprisingly he took the title: Baron Prescott of Kingston upon Hull in the county of East Yorkshire, rather suitable for the distinguished occupant of a substantial detached residence, Addison House in Saltshouse Road.

CHAPTER ELEVEN

REFLECTIONS AND GLIMPSES OF NATIONAL POLITICIANS

Prescott's influence and rise to national prominence were years ahead, but opportunities arose to meet and interview politicians of both the major parties who served in the Cabinet or were members of the Shadow Cabinet.

Denis Healey, the Labour Chancellor of the Exchequer in the late 1970s and a former Defence Secretary, was a popular visitor to Yorkshire Television. A Leeds MP for 40 years, Healey's wit, intellect and approachability created the conditions to guarantee a newsworthy interview.

Sent to York University where Healey was addressing a critical audience of trades unionists opposed to government policy on wage restraint, the Chancellor's humour and repartee put a nervous reporter at ease.

As I'd been told to go to York by ITN whose extremely professional newsdesk recognised the importance of Healey's remarks, I was keen to ensure the quality of the story matched the circumstances.

Any ice was immediately broken when a relaxed Healey found out that he had something in common, however little with myself and the three members of the crew.

"I served in Hull for a short time during the war. What a f...g awful place it was then," he joked.

Turning to me he said: "I hear you know Derek Scott, my personal assistant. He says you'll be kind during the interview."

Whether I was harsh or soft in my questioning didn't matter because such an experienced professional politician as Denis Healey knew precisely which points he would put across and the soundbites that would be used on ITN's early evening news.

Denis Healey

John Smith

Given that the vast majority of stories on regional television were no longer than two and a half minutes, national politicians, like Healey, acquired and required a thorough knowledge of how TV news worked.

I remember being particularly impressed with John Smith, the Labour Leader of the Opposition who died prematurely in May 1994.

On a visit to Lincoln in the late 1980s (when he was Shadow Chancellor) to learn about the problems facing the engineering industry, this eminent Scottish lawyer put over in short sentences the case he was making.

The interview hardly needed any editing; it was a perfect example of how to advocate important points in a limited amount of time.

The Labour Party and the country lost a substantial figure when Smith died at the peak of his powers, and on hearing the shocking news of his death, I recalled his clear and authoritative manner which he had deployed so skilfully.

Potentially, Smith could have become a giant in Labour and British politics; one who can legitimately can be described as such was Roy Jenkins, Chancellor of the Exchequer from 1967-70 in Harold Wilson's administration and Home Secretary twice, 1965-67 and then between 1974-76, also under Wilson.

A passionate enthusiast of the UK's membership of the European Union, Jenkins was appointed to the top job in the EU, president of the Commission, which he held from 1977 to 1981.

Within a few weeks of leaving his EU job, and before he embarked on his campaign to break the mould of British politics by forming the Social Democrats (later the Lib Dems), a Jenkins event surprisingly appeared in the news diary of the Lincoln office of Yorkshire Television.

Lincoln and its area have many attractions, not least the city's magnificent cathedral, but with respect to the district covered from Lincoln, it wouldn't be classified as a hard news patch.

Roy Jenkins former Home Secretary and Chancellor of the Exchequer

So a visit by an international statesman of Jenkins' status was extraordinary.

He had accepted an invitation from Bassetlaw Borough Council to open an industrial estate in Worksop in North Nottinghamshire, quite a contrast to attending G8 conferences of world leaders and having talks in the White House with the President of the USA.

The press were invited to a buffet lunch which followed the opening by Jenkins, and I noticed that he was standing alone with no one to talk to. I'm not saying that he was being shunned by the Labour representatives who controlled the council, after all he'd been invited by them.

But it's fair to say that Jenkins had nothing in common any more with the Labour Party he'd grown up in. The red wine at the buffet was perfectly adequate, but not remotely of the vintage or class that Jenkins was accustomed to; a decent claret or Chateau Lafite was not on offer, but naturally it didn't stop him having a glass.

I'd always admired Jenkins and enjoyed reading the political biographies he'd written and essays on major figures in public life, such as Ernest Bevin, the Foreign Secretary in the post-war Labour Government, and Hugh Gaitskell (Labour Leader 1955-63) with whom Jenkins was close politically and personally.

So as he was alone and staring into space, this was not an opportunity to be missed. After a few pleasant opening remarks, I asked Jenkins if he would mind explaining the high drama in May 1940 which resulted in Winston Churchill becoming Prime Minister at the expense of the floundering Neville Chamberlain.

A political history lesson gradually evolved as Jenkins recounted the famous meeting in Downing Street between Chamberlain, Churchill and Lord Halifax, the Foreign Secretary.

In particular, he emphasised that Chamberlain knew he couldn't continue, that Halifax understood that a peer sitting in the House of Lords could not be Prime Minister, and after a long period of silence it was clear that Churchill would take over and lead the war effort against Hitler.

For 10 or 15 minutes, Jenkins' account of such a vital turning point in British history contrasted sharply with the drab features of a local authority room in Worksop. His brief tutorial, willingly given and presented enthusiastically to a complete stranger, came back vividly 20 years later when I read Jenkins' acclaimed biography of Churchill, published in 2001.

In chapter 30, Through Disaster in the Fjords to Triumph in Downing Street he explains in stimulating detail the historic events which fell Churchill's way enabling him to achieve his career ambition.

Jenkins, naturally, was highly critical of the policies pursued by the Conservative Governments led by Margaret Thatcher, Prime Minister between 1979-91. As a reporter, I never interviewed a Prime Minister, but did chat casually to Harold Wilson during a visit to Leeds once he'd left office, and as a student, following a dinner in Parliament, bought Ted Heath a drink in one of the bars at the House of Commons during his first period as Leader of the Opposition (1965-70).

I had no idea what Heath's tipple was, but expected it to be something stronger than a half of larger and lime. On the other hand, Willie Whitelaw, a future Northern Ireland Secretary and Home Secretary under Heath and Thatcher respectively, enjoyed a whiskey and water.

Heath was stiff and rather cold as we talked whereas Whitelaw, who'd taken me into the nearest bar he could find, one favoured by Labour MPs, couldn't have been more polite.

At the height of Thatcher's power, she was opposed vigorously by Labour led by Neil Kinnock, the Liberals and Jenkins and the SDP

Harold Macmillan –
Prime Minister 1957–63

(Social Democratic Party) which he formed with other prominent Labour politicians. However, the protests she faced were not confined to the Left and Centre-Left.

Indeed, Thatcher's style and determination to overturn the post-war consensus in British politics were condemned by the former Conservative Prime Minister, Harold Macmillan, in power from 1957 to 1963.

Taking the day off from Yorkshire Television newsroom in November 1985 to attend a Conservative dinner at the Royal Overseas League in London, I had an amusing experience involving Macmillan, by now a doddery 91 year old, who was the star speaker.

Supermac may have been fragile, but his mind had retained its sharpness and his humour sparkled.

Rising slowly because of his age and knowing full well the impact his appearance was making, he delivered a fluent and memorable attack on Thatcher's policies, such as selling State owned industries, and their consequences in a calm and quiet tone.

"It's very common with individuals or estates when they run into financial difficulties to find that they have to sell some of their assets. First the Georgian silver goes, and then all that nice furniture that used to be in the saloon. Then the Canalettos go."

As intended, his speech attracted widespread publicity in the national media, but my personal memory was much less to do with the contents of Macmillan's remarks.

At some stage, I was joined in the gents' loo by the former Prime Minister, shuffling with the help of walking sticks, and escorted and propped up by Peter Walker, a former Cabinet Minister, and Julian Critchley MP, a constant critic of Thatcher.

They made sure Macmillan reached the urinal in one piece and stood behind him in case he fell over. I was standing in the next position, thinking it's not every day you pee alongside a former Prime Minister and one as distinguished as Supermac.

But then this extraordinary encounter took an almost comical turn when Critchley, checking to see if his political hero was ready to return to the dining room, asked deferentially:

"Has, sir, finished?"

Macmillan assured Walker and Critchley that he had; they then assisted him to step down from the urinal and held each of Supermac's elbows as he shuffled out of the gents and back safely to his seat in the dining room.

Great relief all round.

CHAPTER TWELVE

THE HILLSBOROUGH DISASTER AND BOXING CLEVER IN SHEFFIELD

One of the benefits of working for Yorkshire Television was that it covered such a big area requiring regional offices in Hull, Grimsby, Lincoln and Sheffield, all of which were staffed by reporters and a camera crew, backed up by a small army of freelance cameramen and women.

I always enjoyed working in Sheffield and South Yorkshire, not least because of the football clubs which were and are a frequent source of news. Sheffield United, Sheffield Wednesday, Doncaster Rovers, Rotherham United, Barnsley and Chesterfield (North Derbyshire) cooperated willingly on a wide range of stories: the sacking of managers, the appointment of a successor, new signings or success in the league and cup competitions.

That kind of news coverage was predictable, but nothing could have prepared anyone for the horrors of the Hillsborough Disaster in April 1989 at Sheffield Wednesday's ground where more than 90 Liverpool supporters were crushed to death.

The hellish scale of the disaster, the worst in UK sporting history, has been repeatedly covered in depth as has the fight for justice and the truth by the families of the Liverpool fans who lost their lives.

Little good can be achieved by regurgitating the circumstances, but I can recall aspects of the build-up to the FA Cup semi-final between Liverpool and Nottingham Forest and the aftermath.

The day before the game, on the Friday, I was the YTV reporter in Sheffield, and the obvious story to cover was how South Yorkshire Police were going to tackle the invasion of the city by thousands of fans.

The senior officer in charge of planning and executing the police operation, before and during the arrival of the supporters, was Chief Superintendent David Duckenfield, then unknown but he instantly became a notorious figure following the catastrophe.

I remember clearly Duckenfield explaining to me how his officers would handle the Liverpool and Forest fans and how they would be kept separate as they arrived and entered the ground.

David Duckenfield

I also recall Duckenfield showing me an outline or chart of his plans and, as he said, police in Sheffield had previously managed FA Cup semi-finals at Hillsborough and, were, therefore, experienced.

We also filmed inside the ground and took shots of the police control room from where Duckenfield would direct the operation as thousands queued to get in.

Everything seemed in order for the following day.

On that Saturday, I was covering a rugby union match for The Sunday Times near Manchester at Heywood Road, the home of Sale RUFC, one of the top sides in the North. As the game ended, a Sale official, who knew I lived in Yorkshire, told me something terrible had happened at Sheffield Wednesday.

"I was there only yesterday. Do you know what's happened?"

"Not in any detail, but people have died."

After filing two reports for The Sunday Times, one for the early edition and the next, a re-write for the later editions, I contacted Yorkshire Television to suggest I drove to Sheffield to help with the coverage of the disaster.

"We are OK for the weekend but go to Sheffield first thing on Monday morning", was the advice from the news desk.

Once there, interviews were quickly arranged with two high ranking officers from South Yorkshire Police. While other reporters followed up many other issues of the disaster, my responsibility was to find out what action the police were now taking; before the interview started the officers asked if I minded having a word with them.

Not at all.

Off the record, they said, our view is that Liverpool fans were responsible, they'd been drinking, they'd arrived late and many travelled without tickets.

These allegations were not repeated in the interview, and were subsequently rejected by the Taylor Report (1990), written by a senior judge, Lord Peter Taylor, who concluded:

"The main reason for the disaster was the failure of police control."

The campaign by the Liverpool families to establish the truth and to attempt to hold to account those responsible for the deaths of 96 people lasted more than 30 years.

In April 2016, a new inquest ruled that the 96 victims had been unlawfully killed and that Liverpool fans were not to blame.

The next stage in the Hillsborough Disaster came in November 2019 when, after a trial lasting seven weeks at Preston Crown Court, David Duckenfield, now 75, was found not guilty of gross negligence manslaughter back in April 1989.

On reflection, reporting from Sheffield was not restricted to covering football stories at the city's clubs. Top class squash, for example, was thriving in the 1980s and remains popular.

An exhibition match by two of the greatest players in the history of squash, Geoff Hunt and Jonah Barrington, attracted much interest and support when it was staged at the Abbeydale club in the affluent suburb of Dore.

Both Hunt, world champion in 1976, 77, 79 and 1980, and Barrington, six times winner of the British Open between 1967 and 1973, may have been past their best, but were still superb players; characterised by endless hours of preparation and training. Their fitness was quite amazing. Throughout the years at the summit of their profession, their bodies had been punished severely as I saw when visiting the changing room after the match.

Both Hunt and Barrington were stretched out on the floor, exhausted and covered in pools of sweat. Hunt, I remember, said it took him at least 20 minutes to recover fully, and in particular, his knee joints had been brutally battered which affected his mobility, though you wouldn't have known it watching him competing against Barrington.

But by the time the tough Australian was in his mid to late 40s, Hunt was able to pace himself without losing any effectiveness or the ability to demonstrate a dazzling array of shots.

Barrington and Hunt were temporary guests in Sheffield and visiting past champions, but across the city in a much poorer area future champions were being produced in a sport that didn't involve hitting a ball, but in hitting your opponent.

The boxing gym at St Thomas' Boys and Girls Club in Wincobank has trained and developed four world champions, all taken to the top by Irishman Brendan Ingle who before his death in 2018 was, without question, one of the most successful trainers/managers in post-war British boxing.

A former professional middleweight, the Dubliner had settled in Wincobank, an area of Sheffield that suffered from its fair share of tearaways; so much so that the local vicar asked Ingle in 1964 what he could do to stop youths and hooligans running wild in the streets.

Ingle's answer was to open a boxing gym in the church hall at St Thomas', but its purpose turned out to be broader than just producing world

Brendan Ingle

champions: cruiserweight Johnny Nelson who fought from 1986-2005, featherweight Prince Naseem Hamed (1992-2002), lightweight Junior Witter (1997-2015) and middleweight Kell Brook (2014-17).

The first time I visited Ingle's gym, he was preparing middleweight Herol Bomber Graham for a fight, Graham (1978-98) is considered to have been one of the most outstanding British boxers never to have won a world title, although he held European, British and Commonwealth titles.

As we watched him train, Ingle explained: "The great thing about this place is that it keeps kids off the streets. When they're boxing, they don't get into trouble and it gives them some discipline."

Brendan's contribution and success in and out of the ring was recognised in 1998 with the award of the MBE for services to boxing and for his work with young people in Sheffield.

It's impossible to quantify how many youngsters Brendan Ingle's gym kept out of trouble because of the values he instilled but may be if he'd been able to influence Paul Sykes, a heavyweight boxer and violent criminal from Wakefield, Sykes would have realized his potential.

In and out of jail for much of his adult life, Sykes fought JL Gardner in 1979 for the British and Commonwealth heavyweight titles at Wembley. Aged 33, he lost in six rounds.

As Sykes prepared for one of his fights as a pro from 1978-80, a news crew from Yorkshire Television filmed his training.

The boxer came over well in the interview I did and answered the questions intelligently, but what sticks in the mind was the comment made to me afterwards by one of Sykes' entourage.

"Paul is very grateful for what Calendar is doing for him because he's had a tough time. If you ever need any help on anything just let me know."

I knew precisely what he meant, but wasn't daft enough to take up the invitation; apart from anything else, I didn't have any enemies who needed seeing to.

Sykes, who died in Wakefield in 2007, aged 60, after a serious illness, could, according to those with boxing expertise, have achieved glory in the ring.

Interestingly his talent was recognised by the American fighter, Leon Spinks, who employed Sykes as a sparring partner.

Spinks caused one of the biggest shocks in boxing history in February 1978 by beating Muhammed Ali at Las Vegas in a contest for the undisputed heavyweight championship of the world. However, he lost the re-match seven months later.

The next sportsman, the greatest ever in his speciality I approached rarely lost, and his presence is still felt at Headingley cricket ground in Leeds more than 70 years since his last appearance.

CHAPTER THIRTEEN

A LETTER FROM SIR DON BRADMAN

Journalism prospers as a result of creative or imaginative ideas whether you are working in newspapers, magazines, broadcasting or the various forms of the internet. One such promising proposal came in the early 1980s.

I was the reporter, scriptwriter and researcher on a series of programmes devoted to cricket, a sport that's revered in Yorkshire and has been for generations. The county is the most successful in terms of winning the County Championship, more than 30 outright titles, and throughout history many players of the highest class have been and are Yorkshire-born and have performed with distinction for Yorkshire and England.

Don Bradman

The list of outstanding cricketers from the county is almost endless; this was reflected in a series called Past Masters, broadcast in 1981.

Yorkshire Television featured: Sir Len Hutton, former England captain, scorer of over 40,000 runs in his first class career between 1934 and 1960. He played in 79 Tests (1937-55), hit 19 Test hundreds and scored 6,971 runs averaging 56.67. Altogether Hutton scored 129 hundreds, and in 1938 set a new record for the highest individual Test score of 364 at the Oval against Australia, a record which lasted for 20 years.

Len Hutton, Don Bradman and David Frith, Cricket Historian

Fast bowler Fred Trueman: 67 Tests (1952-65). 307 Test wickets at an average of 21.57. In his first class career (1949-69), Trueman took 2304 wickets at 18.29. He was the first bowler to reach 300 Test wickets.

Off-spinner Jim Laker: Bradford-born but played for Surrey, famously taking 19-90 in 1956 at Old Trafford against Australia, the highest number of wickets by a bowler in a first class match in cricket history.

Fred Trueman

46 Tests: 1948-59: 193 wickets at 21.24. First class career: 1946-64/65: 1944 wickets average of 18.41.

Jim Laker is the Yorkshire-born cricketer who never played for his native county, the one who got away.

Past Masters paired each of the principal characters with the first class cricketer with whom they formed a successful England partnership.

So Hutton renewed his friendship with his England opening bat, Cyril Washbrook from Lancashire, Trueman was joined by Brian Statham, also of Lancashire, and Laker was interviewed alongside Johnny Wardle (Yorkshire and England spinner) because Laker's Surrey and England colleague, Tony Lock, was unavailable and living in Western Australia.

Not surprisingly, given the popularity of cricket in the YTV transmission area, Past Masters, was well received. Reviews were favourable, and it seemed sensible, if possible, to continue the theme.

At an informal editorial meeting, I suggested writing to Sir Don Bradman, universally accepted as the greatest batsman in the history of cricket who finished his Test career with a batting average of 99.94, the best known of all cricket stats.

The programme idea, a long shot but worth trying, was to reunite the famous Australian with Headingley, the Leeds Test arena where he had enjoyed so many triumphs since his first appearance there in 1930.

Indeed, every time I go to Headingley today to meet Yorkshire cricketers with a view to writing a feature, I instantly think of Bradman's achievements against England.

His run scoring defies belief: in only six innings, he amassed 963 runs at an average of 192.

1930: 334 (309 made on the first day) 1934: 304, 1938: 103 and 16, 1948: 33 and 173 not out.

Bradman scored quickly and was therefore the most popular of entertainers and a super-hero with spectators – his 334, creating a new Test record for the biggest individual Test score, came from only 448 balls.

His last Test at Leeds in July 1948 attracted over the five days a record crowd of 158,000 who were rewarded again as The Don scored yet another century on this occasion 173 not out as Australia chased an improbable 404 to win on the fifth day.

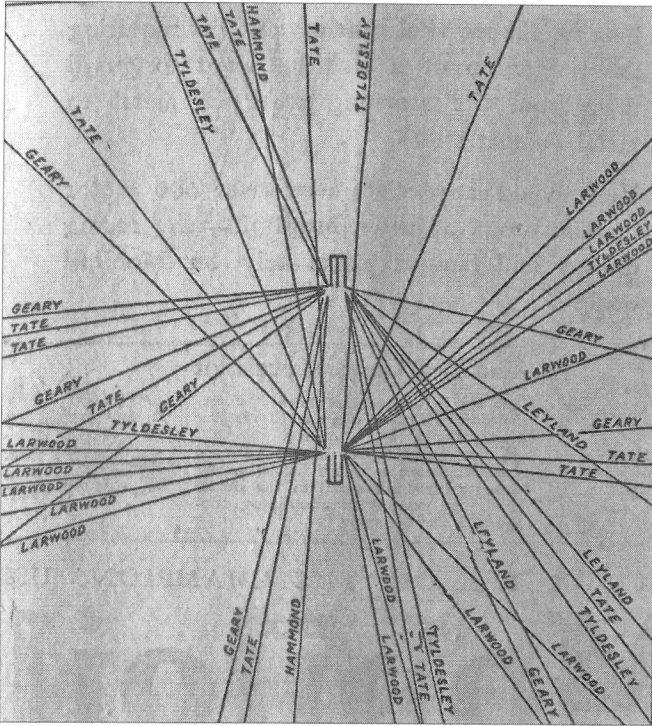

Diagram of Bradman's boundary strokes at Leeds 1930

Presentation of Life Membership Memento to D. G. Bradman

Bradman's permanent impact was inevitably made at other Yorkshire grounds, notably at Bramall Lane in Sheffield and at Scarborough. Indeed, the Australian captain's last three figure score in England, 153- was made at the Scarborough Festival in September 1948.

So great was Bradman's popularity in Yorkshire that shortly after the end of his last game in England, before the Australian team's final tour matches in Scotland, he was given honorary life membership of Yorkshire, the first overseas player to receive that privilege, and presented with a silver salver by the county's president TL Taylor. The ceremony was watched by 14,000 cheering spectators.

In his speech of thanks, Bradman replied:

"I shall never cherish any memory more than the reception in Leeds", referring to his final Test appearance at Headingley.

"Not only was it the greatest I have ever received in this country, but also the greatest I have received from any public anywhere in the world."

So, given this rich background, I wrote to Sir Don Bradman on Yorkshire Television notepaper to inquire if he were willing to take part in a special programme during which he would visit Headingley again and reminisce on his past glories.

We were also keen to reunite Bradman with two Yorkshire and England adversaries, Sir Len Hutton, who'd played in the 1948 Test, and Norman Yardley, the England skipper in the 1948 Ashes series. Yardley also captained Yorkshire from 1948 to 1955.

On paper, the ingredients looked promising in Leeds, but less so in Adelaide where Bradman lived. Within a couple of weeks, he replied courteously, thus providing me with one of my most treasured possessions.

His typed written letter on August 27th 1981 from his home in Holden Street, Kensington Park, South Australia explained why he couldn't accept the invitation:

Dear Mr Williams,

I duly received your letter of the 12th of August and regret some delay in replying due to local problems, but the subject matter was not urgent.

I knew about your feature with Jim Kilburn and Bill Bowes because I correspond with Jim. It is so sad that such a gifted man should be sadly afflicted.

The question you raise is largely academic because I see no likelihood of my going to England again.

At 73 years of age, and after a life which, to paraphrase Mr Fraser, has not been easy, my inclination to travel is diminished. Moreover, I have an inbuilt dislike of personally appearing on T/V. It suits me far better to be a watcher, though I must admit that the speed of scoring of some batsmen in the recent tests made watching questionable entertainment. But then as the only foreigner ever to be made a life member of Yorkshire CCC I suppose I shouldn't criticise Boycott.

I think we must sum up my answer as being in the negative because I am constantly being approached both here and elsewhere to do this sort of thing and frankly I am at the stage of wanting a peaceful existence.

But thank you for your kind thought. I have a very soft spot for Yorkshire and some lovely friends there.

Yours sincerely,

Don Bradman.

Naturally, I was thrilled to receive such a special letter and, frankly, wasn't disappointed because I'd been warned that Bradman, for very good reasons, was a reluctant traveller. It may help if I add some details to the names mentioned in Sir Don's letter.

Jim Kilburn, whom I knew well, was for more than 40 years (1934-1976) the distinguished cricket correspondent of The Yorkshire Post. His elegant style and prose was not only respected by Yorkshire's players from the 1930s to the 1970s, but also by his contemporaries in the press box who acknowledged his national reputation.

Jim Kilburn

An author of several books on cricket, including a History of Yorkshire, cricket lovers, taking The Yorkshire Post, would often turn to Kilburn's columns first in the summer before reading the rest of the paper.

Writing with vast authority and insight, Kilburn's career coincided with the conquering sides of the 1930s led by Brian Sellers who won five Championships before the Second World War and one immediately afterwards in 1946.

Championship titles in 1959, 1960 and 1962 secured by Ronnie Burnett and Vic Wilson were described eruditely, and as Yorkshire's dominance in the 1960s gathered strength under Brian Close (winners in 1963, 66, 67 and 68), Kilburn's stature grew accordingly because a new generation of readers appreciated his experience.

A cricket writer who befriended Yorkshire stars Herbert Sutcliffe, Bill Bowes, Hedley Verity and Hutton and who'd observed Wardle, Willie Watson, Close, Trueman, Ray Illingworth and Geoff Boycott, possessed knowledge given to few.

Sadly in retirement, JM Kilburn's eyesight began to fade, but his blindness, thankfully, did not prevent him contributing splendidly to a Past Masters programme alongside his friend Bill Bowes.

Tall and bespectacled, Bill's fame was earned in the 1930s as Yorkshire's quick and successful opening bowler.

Bill Bowes

A consistent wicket taker who played a significant role in the county winning seven Championships, Bill also played in 15 Tests (1932-1946).

He finished his first class career with 1639 wickets and an average of 16.76, a remarkably low figure and, oddly, took more wickets than he scored first class runs, 1531. But that's not surprising because Bill had little skill with the bat and wasn't the sharpest fielder either.

However, these weaknesses didn't matter; he delivered match winning displays with the ball in Yorkshire sides which dominated the County Championship in the 1930s.

Among many highlights of Bill's career was dismissing Bradman first ball in the Melbourne Test on the 1932-33 Bodyline Tour.

He retired as a Yorkshire player in 1947 and later trained as a journalist writing on cricket for the Yorkshire Evening News and then the Yorkshire Evening Post until 1973.

Wise, intelligent and thoughtful, and kind to me on several occasions, Bill was a lovely man whose visits to Yorkshire Television were always looked forward to.

On one occasion we took Bill out for lunch to a fancy restaurant in Headingley where the menu was chalked on a blackboard.

"Have whatever you want, Bill," I said.

"Well, it all looks very nice, but we are not paying five pounds for a bloody duck," was the reply from our distinguished guest who clearly didn't think it was right to be wasting money on something so frivolous as a duck, however well cooked.

I once made the mistake of asking Bill if his pace at the peak of his career in the 1930s was roundabout the same as that of Chris Old, a Yorkshire and England opening bowler who claimed 1070 first class wickets between 1966 and 1986.

Bill wasn't amused. It was an innocent question. He didn't reply, but if looks could kill. I instantly got the message and moved on to another topic.

Old, when fully fit, was a top class bowler but his career was interrupted by injury, and it clearly upset Bill that I should talk of him in the same breath. It's safe to say that Bill thought players of his generation were made of sterner stuff.

Bradman's letter, before referring to Geoff Boycott, mentions Malcolm Fraser; for those who may have forgotten the history of Australian politics, he was Liberal Prime Minister between 1975-83, and in office when Bradman wrote his reply.

As to Boycott, the Yorkshire and England opening batsman, he deserves a chapter of all his own because of his status.

Sir Don's polite rejection may have stopped Yorkshire Television turning an imaginative idea into a programme of genuine substance, but 40 years on after the invitation to The Don, and more than 70 years after his last Test appearance at Headingley, the standards he set and his records he established still stand – the measure of his unsurpassed greatness.

His 334(1930) remains the highest individual Test score at Leeds, and he is the only batsman in Tests to score two triple hundreds at the ground.

At the time of writing, Bradman is one of only two batsmen to score a century before lunch on the opening day of the Leeds Test.

His letter mentioned that he was the only foreigner to have been made an honorary life member of Yorkshire County Cricket Club. That was certainly true for many years, but subsequently two overseas players, who played for Yorkshire with distinction, the illustrious Indian batsman, Sachin Tendulkar(1992), and the Australian bat, Darren Lehmann(1997-2006), also received the same honour.

Sir Donald Bradman died in February 2001 aged 92, but his presence is still felt at Headingley because his portrait can be seen in the old pavilion.

DG Bradman: Tests: 52. 1928-1948. 6,996 runs. average: 99.94. 29 Test hundreds.

CHAPTER FOURTEEN

AND IN COMES LARWOOD

It's appropriate that a letter from Sir Don Bradman should be followed by memories of Harold Larwood, the legendary Nottinghamshire and England fast bowler from the 1920s and 1930s.

The history and the acrimony of the 1932/33 Bodyline Tour to Australia has been written about endlessly, so little is served by detailed repetition.

In outline, the central issue was that Larwood's single purpose during the sensational series was to destroy the batting genius of Bradman, aided and abetted by Bill Voce, also of Notts.

In the previous Ashes contest in England in 1930, Bradman had wrecked the English bowlers by scoring 974 runs at an average of 139.14, it remains the biggest individual total in a Test series.

Therefore, a plan was devised to stop him. The architect was England's skipper, Douglas Jardine, who instructed his fast bowlers, notably Larwood and Voce, to bowl bouncers directly at Bradman who was surrounded by five or six close-in fielders on the leg side, waiting for a catch if the ball flew uncontrollably off his bat.

The plan worked. Jardine regained the Ashes, Larwood, the spearhead of his attack, took 33 wickets, and Bradman, on the losing side by four Tests to one, was restricted, by his high standards, to only 396 runs (one hundred only). His average fell to 56.57.

Extraordinarily, the opportunity to relive the drama of the Bodyline series, the bitterness almost ruined Anglo-Australian relations, came following a phone call to my desk in the YTV newsroom from Test umpire Dickie Bird.

"Guy lad. Guess who I've just had lunch with? You won't believe it. Harold Larwood and Bill Bowes. Shall I bring them in?"

Clearly, the answer was yes, and in the three hours it took for the three of them to arrive at YTV in Leeds, a studio was quickly found, so that a start could be made on a programme with the eventual title of Fast and Furious-Harold Larwood meets Bill Bowes.

The studio interviews, conducted by Richard Whiteley, were excellent in their content as Larwood, now in his late seventies, explained his rise from a mining village near Nottingham to international fame and controversy.

The use of black and white newsreel film, shot on the Bodyline Tour, illustrated Larwood's terrifying pace and the steep bounce faced by the Australian batsmen as they tried to avoid being hit, not always successfully.

On arrival at the studios in Leeds, I welcomed the fastest and greatest quick bowler of his generation. Larwood's handshake was firm and he looked physically in good shape; he still spoke with a Nottinghamshire accent even though he and his family had lived in Sydney for 30 years.

Of all the twists and turns in Harold's life, the decision to emigrate to Australia, where he was genuinely happy but where his bowling tactics were so vilified, was indeed astonishing.

Almost 50 years on from terrorising Bradman and the Aussie team, Larwood's height, five foot eight, looked the same as it was at his peak. As we walked to the studio, I remember thinking why was it that a man of medium height had been able to generate such pace and bounce.

The short answer was Harold's tough physique. His back, shoulders and arms were naturally strong, initially as a result of the power he'd built up labouring underground in the pit.

Later, following the recording with Bowes and Bird, Larwood relaxed in the hospitality room where the conversation flowed.

While he enjoyed a cup of tea and reminisced about the 1930s, I noticed a bowl of fruit on a table in front of him.

Cheekily, I asked Harold if he'd mind demonstrating how he bowled. Removing his jacket, he rolled up his shirt sleeves and grabbed an apple which instantly turned into a new ball.

Holding the apple with his fingers slightly apart as if there were a seam, Harold moved his wrist forward to show how his out swinger would have been delivered.

The room fell quiet as the most feared fast bowler in England between the wars, calmly and methodically explained his technique.

"And don't forget", he added, "You've got to bend your back."

As Bill Bowes said during the programme: "Harold was the maestro."

Fast and Furious concentrated on the memories of two celebrated fast bowlers, both of whom enjoyed triumphs with England. Larwood's pace stood out from the raw beginnings of his professional career at Nottinghamshire as I found out when I met Willis Walker, a team-mate and consistent run scorer for Notts, who appeared in 405 matches between 1913 and 1937.

At the time of our meeting in the summer of 1986, Willis was the oldest living County Championship cricketer, according to the 1987 Wisden. Then 93, and living in Bingley near Bradford, he described how he first met Larwood at Trent Bridge in 1922.

"I was the first Notts batsman that Harold bowled to when he reported to the nets for a trial. Jim Iremonger, our coach, said:

'Put on your pads, Willis, and see what this boy's like.'

"I batted half an hour against Larwood and when we'd finished I told Iremonger: 'He's very fast off the pitch, but isn't he small?'

"When you'd faced a few overs of him, you realised Harold was out of the ordinary. He was so accurate, with plenty of power in his shoulders."

Just in case anyone of today's generation, whether spectators or first class players, has any doubts as to how dangerous Larwood was, Willis recalled two frightening incidents.

"Harold bowled a bouncer at a Sikh batsman, Joginder Singh, at Trent Bridge in July 1932. It hit him on the head. Blood was pouring out and, as he went down, he said: 'Do not touch me, do not touch me.' We didn't because he felt he was one of the Untouchables and, in fact, it was the 12th man in the Indian side that helped him off the pitch because he was of the same caste.

"And then in a Championship game against Somerset, Harold bowled one which pitched short and the batsman fell over his stumps. The bat flew up in the air. He was so mesmerised that he picked up a stump and thinking it was his bat, he started walking to the pavilion."

My anecdotes are simply glimpses of Larwood and those who feel they need a much more detailed account of his life and career should read the award winning biography by Duncan Hamilton published in 2009.

Larwood, who died in Sydney at the age of 90 in 1995, took 1427 wickets (average 17.51) in a first class career from 1924 to 1938, and in 21 Tests(1926-1933) claimed 78 wickets at an average of 28.35.

Willis Walker (1892-1991) was 99 and nine days when he passed away near Keighley. He scored more than 18,000 runs for Nottinghamshire and with Larwood won the County Championship in 1929.

Harold Larwood – England and Nottinghamshire fast bowler from the 1920s and 1930s … 1427 wickets av: 17.51

Willis Walker – Nottinghamshire batsman and team mate of Larwood

CHAPTER FIFTEEN

MEMORIES OF GEOFF BOYCOTT

Bradman's reference to Geoffrey Boycott in his letter emphasised the need for Test cricket to be entertaining so that spectators got value for money. No one ever doubted Bradman's ability to score quickly and heavily which was why as a selector he preferred batsmen who played positively.

As regards Boycott, awarded a knighthood in September 2019, there is no need whatsoever to reproduce the details of the several crises and conflicts which engulfed the Yorkshire and England opening batsman throughout his controversial career from 1962 to 1986.

Accusations of selfishness and slow scoring at the expense of the team and vivid criticisms of Boycott's behaviour towards others have been recorded countless times, and while many may have suffered or been offended, my dealings with him were perfectly pleasant.

True, Geoff can be blunt, but I also knew where I stood with him, and whether I was working for Yorkshire Television, Sports Illustrated, a Cape Town publication, or The Cricket Paper, he cooperated most professionally.

It is worth reminding ourselves, briefly, the scale of his achievements: 108 Tests (1964-1982) 8114 runs, 22 hundreds batting average of: 47.72.

In a first class career stretching from 1962 until 1986, Boycott scored 48,426 runs, hit 151 centuries in 609 matches and finished with a batting average of 56.83.

A world class bat and at the height of his career, the England batsman was the scalp the opposition's new ball attack wanted to remove above anyone else.

Growing up and as my interest in Yorkshire cricket developed much further, you followed Boycott's progress closely, and I can remember watching his Test debut at Trent Bridge in June 1964 against Australia.

Geoffrey Boycott drives Greg Chappell to complete his 100th century in first class cricket at Headingley against Australia in August 1977

Sir Geoffrey Boycott during his commentary career

Along with a few other boys at Giggleswick, who were also keen Boycott and Yorkshire supporters, I was invited to the chaplain's study to watch him open England's batting for the first time.

Our schoolboy enthusiasm hadn't any limits and nor did our optimism that our Yorkshire hero would be a success. About 60 years later, I can still see Australia's opening pace attack of Graham McKenzie and Grahame Corling running in to bowl at Boycott, wearing glasses. I can still see him, too, stroking a boundary through mid-off on his way to 48 before being dismissed.

Today's television coverage has revolutionised the broadcasting of Test cricket, but back then in the 1960s, the BBC's black and white pictures didn't in any way lessen the tension and the enjoyment which cricket lovers felt, and as you watched Boycott, the BBC's high professional standards picked out his characteristics, total concentration, solid defence, orthodox technique and Geoff's best shot, the back foot punch or square cut through the covers or down towards third man.

His obsession with occupying the crease and ability to reduce errors to a minimum produced a master craftsman; Boycott was, therefore, a natural to present his own coaching programme on Yorkshire Television.

His Master Class, broadcast in the 1980s, illustrated Geoff's commitment to perfection, not least the importance of young cricketers dressing smartly in their kit and looking the part.

Boycott's attention to detail while explaining batting technique was the issue I remember the most; his emphasis on thorough preparation and hard work was also put across forcibly to those he was coaching.

Boycott's endless pursuit to be the best and, moreover, to be recorded in history as a great player who would be remembered fondly by future generations, came sharply into focus again in the summer of 1980.

Towards the end of August and into September, Lord's staged the Centenary Test to mark the 100th anniversary of the first Test played in England at The Oval in 1880 against Australia. More than 200 former England and Australian players were reunited at a grand and nostalgic gathering in which Ashes memories flowed and battles refought, verbally.

Unfortunately, the Centenary Test was ruined by rain; at least 10 hours of play were lost in the first three days. As a contest, it ended in a flat draw, although there were some notable performances, particularly by Australia.

Opener Graeme Wood scored 112 in their first innings, but Australia's batting star in both innings was Kim Hughes, 117 followed by a sparkling 84.

As regards England, Boycott top scored with 62 followed by 128 not out in the second innings as England showed no interest in chasing 370 to win in about six hours at a run a minute.

Geoffrey Boycott

With England intent on avoiding defeat, the circumstances suited Boycott's mentality to survive and avoid taking any risks. His application was rewarded as he completed his sixth hundred against Australia, his 19th in all Tests, and during the 252 balls he faced, he overtook the Test aggregate of both Sir Len Hutton (6971) and Sir Donald Bradman (6996).

On an individual basis, the Centenary Test was a personal triumph for Boycott, a story that required following up by the Yorkshire Television news room. On his return home, I arranged for him to be interviewed live on Calendar (YTV's evening news programme) and wrote the script relating to his century at Lord's in the Test to celebrate cricket history.

As soon as Geoff arrived, I showed him the script and congratulated him on his performance. Boycott's reply summed up exactly what made him tick as a professional cricketer and why he'd climbed right to the top.

"Before the game, I did some research and looked at the score card from the first Test and noticed that the great WG Grace had scored a hundred(152) and I was determined to do the same a hundred years later."

No one should be surprised at Boycott's method or single mindedness because they'd been on public view since making his Yorkshire debut in 1959 in the Minor Counties and Second X1 competitions.

His dedication to scoring hundreds and the highest standards of professionalism Geoff demonstrated were praised in some detail in a talk in Hull to the East Riding Cricket Society by Colin Cowdrey, the former Kent and England captain; one of the most skilful of post-war batsmen and himself the scorer of 100 first class centuries (107), Cowdrey appeared in 114 Tests scoring 7624 runs and 22 hundreds.

I attended Cowdrey's meeting both as a journalist and a cricket enthusiast and because he'd be an excellent interviewee and entertaining speaker, I wasn't disappointed.

Knowing that his audience were keen Yorkshire supporters, it made sense for him to make favourable comments about Boycott; in my opinion they ring true today as they did in the 1970s.

"Geoff has made himself into a great player by hard work and constant practice. I wouldn't regard him as a natural because, in my view, his wrists are not supple. That's not a criticism. But what he has achieved is manufactured by hard work and then more hard work."

Once he had retired as a player, Boycott's second career as a media star, whether on television, radio or in newspapers, took off, probably at a faster rate than he scored. Whether you agreed or not with his caustic comments on an England performance, Geoff's outspoken opinions more often than not made cricket sense and were expressed so strongly and simply that viewers, listeners and readers got the message instantly.

Boycott entertained too but, above all else, spoke with convincing authority because of his Test career, his expert knowledge of that era and also of the contemporary scene. He wasn't slow either in giving credit when it was merited.

I was reluctant a bit to approach Geoff for an interview on current issues in case contracts with media companies prevented him doing so; but 40 years on from his most famous and emotional innings, becoming the first player in cricket history to score his 100th first class century in a Test

(August 1977 at Headingley against Australia), I rang him on behalf of The Cricket Paper.

"I'll have to rearrange my schedule to fit you in. Give me a ring back in half an hour and I'll tell you what's happening."

The Cricket Paper was told the signs were hopeful, and the editor said he'd find space in next week's issue for a feature spread over two pages. Quite a showing.

In fact, I didn't need to ring Boycott back. He rang me:

"Right, I've rearranged things. Get yourself over here at 10.00 on Saturday morning and you've got half an hour."

It helped that he lived no more than 20 minutes away from our village near Tadcaster, and Boycott's home on the main street in Boston Spa was a prominent building and, therefore, easy to spot.

Relaxed and chatty, the 30 minutes soon passed by and extended into an hour and a half as Geoff recounted and replayed, if you like, the most memorable innings of his career in front of thousands of natural Boycott supporters.

"I was nervous but after about 25 minutes I felt great and the ball was hitting the middle of the bat. I was in control and got into a cocoon of concentration and nothing bothered me. The odds were huge that I'd get a 100 in the Test, but if I got in, everyone was expecting me to do so. I knew the crowd were with me and that added to the stress and tension.

"I batted in sections: getting off the mark, getting to 10 and then 20. I didn't get too far ahead of myself, but I always batted to score hundreds. I knew Greg Chappell, the Australian captain, was going to put himself on because the main bowlers hadn't got me out.

"I picked three areas where I was going to hit it because they were safe and I've always believed if you get into the 90s, there should be no thing as being nervous. You've been batting for a few hours and should be in control.

"Chappell bowled it just outside the off-stump at the Kirkstall Lane End and I hit it past the stumps on the other side. The ball was half way down the pitch and I knew I was going to hit it and where.

"It's a magical moment that happens only a few times in your career when you know exactly what you are going to do before you've done it.

"It was the best moment in my career, something historic that hadn't been done before."

Needless to say, I was delighted with the contents of Boycott's interview, not least because against my expectations, for some reason he had found extra time to thoroughly explore an outstanding event in post-war British sport whose 40th anniversary required a proper reflection.

CHAPTER SIXTEEN

THE RISE OF ROTHERHAM RUGBY CLUB

Professionally, I've had a lot of fun writing on cricket and rugby union, and my personal view is that a thorough training in news reporting where you must be able to spot a story should help to make a journalist a good sports reporter.

The introduction of competitive leagues in rugby union in the late 1980s transformed English club rugby as it enabled teams to reach the top on merit. Exeter Chiefs being one outstanding example.

Promotion and relegation meant that each match counted, and in the North of England where I lived, it's hard to think of a club that benefited more from this competitive revolution than Rotherham who famously became the first Yorkshire club to appear in the Premiership by winning promotion in the early summer of 2000.

The rise of Rotherham from nowhere to national prominence, and the media coverage that followed, was remarkable considering that the South Yorkshire industrial town, where steel and coal mining once dominated, never possessed a strong rugby union heritage.

Rotherham in rugby terms was not South Wales in the North. The region's football teams, Sheffield Wednesday, Sheffield United, Barnsley, Rotherham United, Doncaster Rovers and Chesterfield ruled the roost as regards mass support and media interest.

Rapid promotions from 1989 to the mid-1990s coincided with my period as a freelance reporter working on Saturdays for Yorkshire on Sunday, published in Bradford. Rotherham's progress was turning into a much stronger story and required wider coverage than that provided by the Rotherham Advertiser, the successful weekly paper.

So a fixture against Durham City in National Five North in March 1994 presented itself as a good opportunity to check on Rotherham's standing and with it the offer to cover the game also for two papers in the North East, The Journal and the Sunday Sun.

During a one sided match, Rotherham thrashed Durham 76-3, scoring 11 tries, an easy win that helped to guarantee another promotion.

I now had to write and then phone my copy through. At this time, I did not own a small portable computer and newspapers still employed copytakers who would write down your words and then send the story to the sports desk for editing. This visit was the first of dozens I made to Rotherham Rugby Club over the next 25 years and produced the first of many amusing moments as I reported regularly on the team's home and away games for The Yorkshire Post, and The Star and Green 'Un in Sheffield.

As Rotherham were promoted to the top league, the Premiership, I also earned commissions from The News of the World and The Sun, two papers owned by Rupert Murdoch.

As I walked into the bar in the clubhouse after the Durham match looking for somewhere to write, I noticed someone sitting precariously on a stool enjoying a drink, probably not his first.

"Sorry to bother you. My name is Guy Williams from Yorkshire on Sunday. Do you know where I can write my match report and is there a phone?"

"And I'm Pernod Pete. I'm the only Anglo-Catholic in Rotherham and one of the few Conservatives in the town," he slurred.

"You're very welcome. Write in the corner over there. No one will bother you."

At this point, Pernod Pete almost toppled over but I prevented him falling in a heap by grabbing his hand. He didn't spill a drop either of his favourite tipple. Over the next few years, Peter Hind became a regular and talkative companion in the bar after games, and I never imagined I'd ever discuss over a pint or two what was wrong with the Church of England in Peter's view, the Roman Catholic doctrinal stance on Mass or the quality of priests in Rotherham's Anglican churches.

Deep theological discussions had their place, but I was more concerned about covering the rapid progression of an ambitious club which had never been part of Yorkshire's Rugby Establishment, and one that was keen to smash traditional barriers and expand its horizons nationally by aiming for the top.

Rotherham's vision was driven by Mike Yarlett, a local businessman and former player, who ran Yorkshire Windows, a thriving company based in the town. Short and stocky and proud of his Rotherham roots, Yarlett's sharp brain when it came to rugby and business combined with direct speaking ensured that the club's interests came first.

Mike Yartlett as a Rotherham player

Mike Yarlett Rotherham benefactor

As he recruited the right players and coaches, Rotherham overtook established clubs like Wakefield, Leeds and Otley and, indeed, famous national sides such as Coventry, Rosslyn Park or Moseley. Certainly in Yorkshire, understandable jealousy arose, but once rugby officially declared itself a legitimate professional sport after the 1995 World Cup, Yarlett and his club took full advantage of the new era.

A combination of local players, signings from Yorkshire clubs and recruits from UK sides and overseas, produced squads that mixed easily off the pitch, but, importantly, delivered results on it.

Without Yarlett's money and his ability to attract decent players who bought into his vision, Rotherham would never have been able to contest the promotion play-off in the late spring of 2000 when memorably they beat, over two legs, Bedford, one of the best clubs in the East Midlands and one with an illustrious history.

Rotherham folk by nature are not fanciful and it's accurate to say that no one at Clifton Lane, the club's small ground, thought that life in the Premiership would be comfortable.

The squad's commitment, hard work and enthusiasm were never questioned, but the Yorkshire club struggled to compete and in their first season in the Premiership won only twice in 22 league games, beating London Irish and Saracens, both at Clifton Lane.

Over the course of a stressful and bruising campaign, Rotherham's weaknesses in attack and defence were apparent as they scored only 29 tries and let in 103. Without the resources or experience of top class clubs, like Northampton, Leicester, Gloucester or Bath, sides with a long and successful history, Rotherham were out of their depth. Heavy defeats, for example, losing 68-12 to Bath and 50-17 at Gloucester, illustrated the chasm between the Premiership and National One.

It was typical of Rotherham's character that their ambition to succeed in the Premiership or at least to regain their place was not destroyed by the punishment handed out in the 2000-01 season. Back in National One again, the club won the title again and with it promotion once more, but if their first campaign had been painful, the second was brutal. Not one match was won. Twenty two defeats, for instance Leicester Tigers hammered them 75-13 and Bath won 47-3, highlighted the increasing and widening gap between the elite and aspiring clubs, even those with wealthy benefactors.

Rotherham scored 32 tries and conceded 90, and were relieved collectively by the return to National One, but the club financially was struck by a crisis and had to be rescued by two Rotherham businessmen, Nick Cragg and Martin Jenkinson.

On reflection, no match illustrated more clearly Rotherham's thrilling rise to the top of English rugby, however brief, than the memorable visit to South Yorkshire by Harlequins, the very essence of rugby union's Establishment. Blazers, Cavalry Twills, regimental and old boys' ties were rarely seen in the Rotherham clubhouse, but they were on a Saturday in January 1997 when the London side appeared at Clifton Lane in the sixth round of the Pilkington Cup, then the RFU's principal knock-out competition.

The biggest crowd in Rotherham's history, 4,000, packed into Clifton Lane, the vast majority hoping to observe an upset. In the build-up to the game, the major talking point had been the presence of Will Carling, the ex-England captain, now captaining Quins. Once the Golden Boy of English rugby and rumoured to have enjoyed a relationship with Diana, the Princess of Wales, Carling's celebrity status was guaranteed not only to attract a substantial crowd but plenty of caustic comment as well.

Will Carling

Capped 72 times by England and captain in 59 internationals, Carling was unquestionably the biggest rugby personality to have played at Clifton Lane. As expected, off the field he conducted himself perfectly, signing dozens of autographs and willingly posing for photographs, and on the field, the England and Quins centre, who'd led his country to three Grand Slams in 1991, 1992 and 1995 and in the final of the 1991 World Cup, demonstrated his hardness and class as Rotherham rose to the challenge.

Early in the first half, Carling was toppled by a ferocious tackle, "Welcome to fucking Rotherham Carling," shouted a delighted and partisan Rotherham supporter. No one could find fault with the team's attitude. Competitive throughout against a Quins team fielding eight internationals, they fought back from 32-9 to score two converted tries, cutting Quins' lead to 32-23. Carling's team, though, possessed more than enough class and power to prevent an upset and eventually won by 42-23, but in defeat by five tries to two, Rotherham advanced their reputation as, indeed, did Carling whose attitude in all aspects was praised without reservation.

The importance of the cup-tie resulted in extensive media coverage, especially from national newspapers which in their match previews had contrasted the background of Carling – Sedbergh, England and Quins with that of Rotherham's skipper who'd grown up in circumstances in Sheffield that were, shall we say, less posh.

Dudley, a tall and rampaging back row forward, was a genuine character, as hard as Sheffield steel, liked a few pints and before a game often enjoyed a cigarette and a mug of tea as he leaned against the rugby posts near the clubhouse. However, once the game started, Dudley smashed into opponents and as Rotherham made rapid progress through the leagues, his performances proved to be hugely influential. Making more than 100 league appearances, he was easily Rotherham's best known player, a feared opponent, the supporters' most popular player and, more than anyone else, signified the club's climb from the bottom to the top.

I shall always remember the photograph of Dudley, arms raised in triumph, taken instantly at the end of the Bedford-Rotherham match at Goldington Road where the Yorkshire team remarkably won promotion to the Premiership in the spring of 2000, the club's proudest moment.

But back to the clash against Harlequins: so big was the media interest that it was impossible to accommodate all the visiting journalists into the small area reserved for the two or three regular reporters.

John Dudley Rotherham forward celebrating promotion to the Premiership in 2000 after beating Bedford – 207 appearances

Instead and much to the amusement of the national press, the club borrowed for the match an open top double decker bus which was parked in a corner of the ground. The view from the top deck was perfect and far better than the view of the games I reported on for more than 20 years.

Given the significance of Carling's visit and the possibility of a cup upset, my space in the Green 'Un, the sports paper circulating in South Yorks, North Notts and North Derbyshire on Saturday nights and published within an hour of games finishing, was more than usual.

First published in 1907, the Green 'Un became a sporting institution in the Sheffield areas for 106 years until it ceased publication in 2013. The distinctive newspaper was as famous as the football clubs it covered in such detail, and for many thousands of football supporters over several generations, buying the Green 'Un at tea time on Saturday evenings was as normal as going to a match.

Unlike reporters covering Sheffield's clubs or Barnsley, Rotherham United, Doncaster Rovers and Chesterfield, my space was small in comparison, but the tasks were the same; phoning the teams through before kick-off, some paragraphs during the first half, the score at half time, extra second half copy and finally an intro and another paragraph plus score and scorers at the end of the match, on the whistle was the term and the order issued by the sports desk.

Rugby union was editorially of much less significance than league football attracting thousands to Hillsborough or Bramall Lane in Sheffield and my work was less stressful than the journalists on The Star in Sheffield covering live soccer. Their reports were so detailed and involved phoning umpteen paragraphs at regular intervals.

I loved phoning copy through during a game and chatting to the army of copytakers. Among my favourites, wearing a phone headset at the paper's office in Sheffield, was Renee who'd been taking copy at the Green 'Un for many years. Renee was still working on Saturday afternoons in her eighties when I began reporting for the paper in the mid-1990s.

At one particular match, I was struggling to get my first paragraph right for the match report when I phoned in after about 20 minutes of action.

"Look luv, all our teams whether it's Wednesday or United always get off to a cracking start. Just say that Rotherham did and you'll be fine."

Which is what we did. No one complained and the copy looked satisfactory when I bought the Green 'Un on my way home to Leeds. That was the pleasing point about the paper. Less than an hour of the match ending, a convoy of vans left the paper's office and drove at speed to deliver the Green 'Un throughout South Yorkshire and across the border into Notts and Derbyshire to shops and garages who sold it. As well as match reports on the professional clubs, there were also reports on amateur sides, features on a range of sports and many excellent pictures.

I loved writing for the Green 'Un and as a reporter, I got a special thrill seeing my report in the paper a short time after it had been phoned over. I'm not claiming any qualities, but you had to be alert, write to length (stick to the word or paragraph count) and be aware of the deadline. The paper's production team were first class and not being a production journalist, I was always amazed at their professionalism and speed which enabled the publication of a top class paper within such a short time.

The coverage of football was never less than first rate. The features, put together in mid-week, were informative, and the dozens of stories, and in particular the pictures of local teams and players in all sorts of sports, were outstanding examples of provincial journalism at its best. South Yorkshire and its border was well served by the Green 'Un, but as with other newspapers in the digital age, sadly, its demise was inevitable.

Its closure ended a way of life for many journalists, but also for readers at home and overseas. Certainly in my period covering Rotherham rugby for the Green 'Un, and the same thoroughness applied to football reporting, BBC local radio, BBC regional television and ITV and Sky never approached its breadth of coverage in my opinion. I can't speak on behalf of football fans as to their views on national and provincial newspapers, but I can say that The Rugby Paper has filled the hole created by the closure of Saturday evening sports papers.

While TRP is not on the streets once a game has finished, its availability on Sundays and match reports from many rugby union leagues up and down the country show the importance of a paper that tackles topical issues. Rugby union fans across the UK are well served, and because TRP is a national publication and one that is specialised, it can devote much space to match coverage which other Sunday papers can't provide.

Once I'd filed my Green 'Un report or a Sunday paper needing copy on a Saturday evening, I'd make sure I had a drink for at least an hour.

Chatting to players, coaches, supporters and match officials was always fun and essential. In my case, working for The Star, The Yorkshire Post or freelancing for another regional paper like the Western Daily Press (Bristol) or the Western Morning News (Plymouth), you had to come up with an angle for Monday's paper. Players and coaches were helpful in my experience. Big names like Carling, Dean Richards (ex-England player and coach at Leicester Tigers, Quins and Newcastle Falcons) and Rob Andrew, the former Wasps and England fly half who also coached at Newcastle, were happy to cooperate once a match had finished and were aware of the media's demands.

Sir Ian McGeechan – Head coach of the British and Irish Lions 1989, 1993, 1997 & 2009.

Similarly, Sir Ian McGeechan, knighted in 2010. The former British and Irish Lions coach, who's from Leeds, and a major international figure, could not have been more helpful in stories for television, newspapers and magazines. An outstanding player with Headingley, Scotland and the Lions, McGeechan's quiet and methodical style combined with his deep knowledge and enthusiasm for the Lions, turned the former Leeds teacher into a formidable coach who achieved glittering success at club and international level.

As this is being written, no one has been appointed Head Coach of the Lions more times than Sir Ian. In 1989, 1993, 1997 and 2009, McGeechan directed operations in Tests against Australia, New Zealand and South Africa-winning series in Australia in 89 and against South Africa in 97.

In terms of personal publicity, Sir Ian's media coverage concentrated on his achievements as the Lions' coach, but it should not be forgotten that he won trophies in club rugby with London Wasps winning the Heineken Cup in 2007, that's the most prestigious European competition, and then the English Premiership in 2008.

In case you're confused that a Yorkshireman played rugby for Scotland and, indeed, coached the national team which famously won the Grand

Slam in 1990 by beating England 13-7 at Murrayfield, it's worth explaining that Sir Ian chose to play for Scotland in honour of his father, Bob, who was from Govan near Glasgow; a proud Scot who served with the Argyll and Sutherland Highlanders during the Second World War.

McGeechan's rugby career as a player, coach and commentator for newspapers and the broadcast media is well known; less known is his love of cricket, and if his rugby had not taken up so much of his time in winter and summer, he may well have achieved his goal of playing for Yorkshire as a professional, in his case a left arm quick bowler who also batted to a decent standard.

A natural sportsman whose primary school in Leeds was no more than a mile from Headingley cricket ground, it was therefore not surprising that as a youngster hours and hours were spent playing cricket on the cobbled streets in the Kirkstall area of Leeds in the 1950s.

In the April issue of The Cricketer magazine in 2019, Sir Ian explained his enthusiasm for the game in what I thought was a revealing interview.

"Every minute in the school yard we played cricket and I'd be playing cricket at five or six years old. The challenge was to stay in on the cobbled streets because the ball was coming in at all sorts of angles. After school about half a dozen of us would walk up to Headingley because at four o'clock they'd open the gates so we could watch the last two hours of the Test.

"We sat on the boundary edge and you had a fair chance of picking the ball up and throwing it back. We used to watch Yorkshire as well and growing up my hero was Brian Close. Closey

Sir Ian McGeechan

was hard as nails and I recall seeing that phot of him in 1963 when he was black and blue after being hit by Wes Hall and Charlie Griffith.

"So cricket was my first love. Rugby came later and holidays in Bridlington were spent playing Tests on the beach. I tried to copy Fred Trueman's action and dragged my foot like him but my mum told me off because I ended up with toes coming out of my shoes.

"My Maths master at secondary school, Ken Dalby, loved cricket and knew Bill Bowes of Yorkshire and England. Ken asked Bill to watch me at school and on the back of that, I was invited to the Yorkshire nets. I was at the nets for three years and was therefore in the Yorkshire system. I'd get the train and bus to Bradford Park Avenue where Yorkshire's coach, Arthur Mitchell, would assess you all the time.

"Arthur was clever because he'd make you bowl to top class batsmen like Close, Doug Padgett and Geoff Boycott. Geoff used to stay longer. He'd say...I want you to bowl at my off stump, I want you bowling short of a length. If you got it wrong you'd know about it but as a kid, it was a privilege to bowl to an England opener.

"I came across Geoff Boycott again when I was selected for the Yorkshire Owls, a Sunday side made up of county players and good league cricketers. He was then playing for England and often batted through the 40 overs. But in one match he got out early and when we went in for tea, Geoff said he wanted to open the bowling and I opened at the other end.

"So that is my claim to fame. That I opened with Boycott, but not the batting."

Sir Ian's technical knowledge of the complexities of rugby union is more than matched by the officials who have to interpret the laws during a match. Trying to be as accurate as possible in my reporting reminds me of an amusing incident involving Rotherham and Wayne Barnes, then very much an inexperienced referee but one whose talent had been recognised by the RFU who'd decided to push his career forward.

As a 21 year old, and a trainee barrister, Barnes had officiated at a Rotherham league game quite early in his refereeing career. It was one of his first assignments at a senior level. After the match, I noticed him standing in the clubhouse and asked if I could check a decision of his that I needed to mention in my copy for Monday's papers.

Our helpful conversation was spotted by Yarlett who was enjoying a drink at the bar, so when I joined him he was eager to find out what I had been talking to Barnes about. I explained, but Yarlett was still not convinced that Barnes had made the right decision.

"You can go back to Wayne Barnes and tell him to stick to barristering because he can't ref."

A quick witted remark that had Yarlett's friends at the bar in stitches. Mike Yarlett's a generous man, and is devoted to rugby's values, and will no doubt have been delighted with Barnes's rapid progress since he reffed that league game in South Yorkshire.

His skill, decision making and rapport with the players forged an outstanding career in professional sport. As I write, Barnes was named World Rugby's Referee of the Year in 2019, has officiated in 100 Test matches, three quarter finals in the World Cup, a semi-final and two bronze finals and he's still barristering in London.

Rotherham's ability to attract the very best referees, those right at the top internationally, continued several years later as the club tried to boost its finances by putting on dinners at which the main speaker was a famous rugby personality.

Wayne Barnes is, as I write, the best known English referee but with a large international reputation, just like Welshman Nigel Owens, arguably the most illustrious British referee.

Amusing, charming, tough and fair, this fluent Welsh speaker who refereed his 100th international during the autumn of November 2020, officiated in the final of the 2015 World Cup, is every inch a personality in his own right just like the stars he's judging.

Invited to Rotherham to speak, he spoke brilliantly about his experiences in rugby's major competitions, but brought the house down at the same time. Owens began his speech in Welsh and chatted in his native tongue for at least a minute. No one in the dining room had a clue what he was talking about, prompting one of the ex-players to say:' Can't he speak English. I don't understand Welsh.'

Wayne Barnes –
Refereed his 100th international
in November 2022 and the
2023 World Cup Final

Suddenly, Owens switched to English.

"I suppose you want to know what I was saying in Welsh.

"I said that the two Rotherham directors I was sitting next to and talking to were the most boring people I've ever met."

Everyone erupted and saw the joke. Owens then gave a witty and informative speech on his career which was received with loud applause when he'd finished.

A television presenter, Owens fully understands the needs of the media and was quite happy before the dinner to chat to me about the pressure of refereeing internationals at home and overseas. Before the introduction of bonus points into the Six Nations in 2017, Owens had advocated the system and its benefits during the interview for The Rugby Paper.

A referee with vision therefore, and a match official who understands players and, just as importantly, when ticket prices are so expensive, knows instinctively that Tests must consider the interests of spectators who would prefer to be entertained.

Clifton Lane home of Rotherham Titans RUFC

Rotherham playing Wharfedale at Clifton Lane

CHAPTER SEVENTEEN

MY YORKSHIRE

Covering cricket and rugby, and writing up interviews with distinguished persons in both sports, has given me much satisfaction, but later in my professional career, I stumbled across an opportunity which stretched my mind in fields other than sport.

Writing for The Yorkshire Post since the mid-1990s introduced me to the paper's lively and lavishly illustrated magazine which is published with Saturday's edition. Opening the magazine and reading it, its strength is not only the range of topics covered, but also the rich talent in many walks of life in this part of the North of England. Yorkshire's grandeur, whether it's industrial reflecting Victorian England, or the beauty of the Dales and the coast, is portrayed at its best in the magazine.

England's largest county combines both its past and present successfully, so if it's Roman or Viking history that is of interest, visit York, or if you want to escape from the industrial and commercial stress of working in Leeds or South Yorkshire, explore the countryside of the Yorkshire Dales or the North York Moors.

As previously mentioned, Hull and the Yorkshire coast have special attractions and as with other areas of the region, their populations possess characteristics shaped by the past, but simultaneously, Yorkshire's districts are building for the future in so many activities; business, leisure and tourism, the arts, sports, charities and politics.

At the front of the magazine, the My Yorkshire feature gives the reader the opportunity to hear from prominent people who have made or are making a name for themselves in a wide range of occupations. What they all have in common is their Yorkshire background, and it doesn't matter if the interviewee was not born in Yorkshire, but obviously the figures agreeing to take part either live or work in the county.

The My Yorkshire personalities have several things in common: their love for the county, its features and contrasts, the respect for the traditional qualities of Yorkshire people, direct and, at times, wounding and blunt speaking, hard work, warmth and friendliness, common sense and caution with money.

These attributes may well stand out, but what's also noticeable is that many of the people I spoke to were complimentary about the opportunities created in Yorkshire from which they've benefited; whatever your walk of life, it's possible to make a success of it in Yorkshire where the quality of life for you and your family can be more enjoyable than London and its suburbia.

The following examples of My Yorkshire interviews give a flavour of the variety the region has to offer: actress Gaynor Faye, star of the ITV drama Emmerdale, Robin Wraith, head chef at Martin House, the first children's hospice in the North at Boston Spa near Leeds, Kim Leadbeater, the sister of the murdered Labour MP Jo Cox killed in June 2016, and Lord Patel from Bradford, the first Asian to be appointed to be a member of the England and Wales Cricket Board.

Lord Patel – Controversial chairman of Yorkshire CCC from November 2021 to March 2023

I decided the best and briefest way in which to hear from the above was to let them describe their first memory of Yorkshire. After the four above, I also include a selection of other My Yorkshire personalities who have contributed much to the region.

Gaynor Faye

Actress Gaynor Faye: "I grew up in the West Park area of Leeds and have happy memories of school. I also have clear memories of visiting Whitby with my sister Yvonne when I was three or four. We stayed as a family on a campsite, and we'd spend hours on the beach with our deckchairs, picnics and buckets and spades.

"Yorkshire now is much more multi-cultural than it was and that's fantastic. What's also a big achievement is that Channel 4 has chosen Leeds as its new headquarters. My mother, Kay Mellor, the television dramatist, backed the move and she's ecstatic."

Chef Robin Wraith: "I was brought up in Bingley near Baildon Moor and I have many happy memories of Bradford, but my happiest memories are of holidays at Sandsend on the Yorkshire coast. We'd go there regularly, playing cricket on the beach and building sandcastles. My time at Bingley Grammar School was enjoyable but my forte came when I went to catering college in Bradford. My grandmother was a great baker and I baked with her; that's where it came from.

"Yorkshire people have sheer grit. That is instilled into the Yorkshire families who come to Martin House. Their world is turned upside down when a child is diagnosed with a terminal illness or dies suddenly. You look at their faces and you see the determination as they live through harrowing experiences. I also think Yorkshire is well known for the hospitality of its people."

Community campaigner Kim Leadbeater and now Labour MP for Batley and Spen, her sister's constituency.

"I'm fortunate to have a lot of positive memories from our childhood in Heckmondwike. I remember going shopping with Jo to Woolworth's in the town centre and buying Pick and Mix sweets. We had lovely family trips to the coast and to places like Brimham Rocks and spent many happy times with our grandparents who lived in Heckmondwike.

"Personally I've always found Yorkshire to be a positive and friendly place, but since Jo was killed, it highlighted that we are not a county free of issues or trouble. What I have found is the strength of Yorkshire people coming together in the face of tragedy."

Lord Patel: "A bit of background first. I was born in Nairobi in 1960 but we had to leave when I was one. My father had a sister in Bradford, so we landed there. We had nothing and lived in a one bedroom back to back in Cobden Street in Queensbury. We had no bathroom and had an outside toilet. You knew you were different because everyone else was white. I didn't go to school until I was seven and didn't read or write until I was eight or nine. My first memories are of playing cricket with a bat made from a wooden milk crate.

"I've seen Bradford on a rollercoaster ride. In the early 1980s, it was a happening place. Bradford was thriving and even before that. But it has suffered with the loss of the textile trade and bad political leadership. Leeds, though, has taken off as a city and everyone thinks about it. However, Bradford is, I think, on an upward trend and we are seeing businesses coming here. I think Yorkshire will be the real Northern Powerhouse if we can get our act together. It's the biggest county, our cities offer different things and I think the future is really bright."

Dancer Sharon Watson: At the time of our interview in late summer of 2016 she was the artistic director of the acclaimed Phoenix Dance Theatre in Leeds.

"My first memories are of growing up in the Harehills area of Leeds. My parents came from different parts of Jamaica and flew to the UK in the 1950s. We had a large family. I was one of eight, so the house was a bit congested. We spent a lot of time outside making bogies and putting the wheels on. We played games and chased around the streets. My mother was a nurse and worked every hour God sent. My first dance lesson was at Harehills Middle School and I so enjoyed it that I knew that was what I wanted to do. I told my parents that I was going to London to train to become a professional dancer. It was tough going to London aged 16, but I had family down there and I took my sister with me.

"I think Yorkshire is changing for the better. You look at the landscape in Leeds which is now an attractive and a good place to bring up a family. I admire the drive that is going on in Yorkshire. Culture has a keen part to play and I'm hoping that Leeds can be nominated in 2023 to be the European Capital of Culture for that year. We need to shout about Yorkshire culture and we are looking beyond Leeds to places like Bradford and Halifax to feed into what we are trying to do."

Johnny Whiteley MBE: Johnny was one of the best sportsmen to have been produced by Hull. A top class rugby league player, he played more than 400 times for Hull FC and as Great Britain coach won the Ashes in Australia.

Johnny Whiteley

"I was born near the Hull fish docks. My father was a trawlerman. We lived in Scarborough Street and one of my first memories was when we were bombed in May 1942. I was in the air raid shelter and when we came out half our house had disappeared. We had to live in hostels and church halls and slept on mattresses stuffed with straw. The bomb killed 50 people and injured 200 odd.

"We've had bad periods in Yorkshire because of the economic climate. The mines have shut and here in Hull the fish docks have closed, but I would say, overall, the region has changed for the better. People are living in better housing and they expect more than we did in the back streets. People are better educated. I left school at 14 and got a job as a fish filleter."

Katherine Brunt: Katherine is one of England's best female cricketers, winning three World Cups and as a successful fast bowler has been the Women's Cricketer of the Year, chosen by the England and Wales Cricket Board, four times.

"I grew up in Dodworth near Barnsley, and remember making a cup of tea with my mother when I was four years old. As for cricket, my first competitive game was at Shaw Lane, home of Barnsley Cricket Club. I'd have been eight. I've still got my first bat which was homemade. My dad, who was a miner for 25 years and my brother Daniel, taught me how to play.

"I think things have got better in Yorkshire and particularly the willingness to talk about mental health issues. Now, you can speak to someone whereas before problems would get worse, mental health was ignored, you just got on with it and didn't talk about things. I believe there are more opportunities for females in sport. When I was growing up, I was the only girl around playing cricket. Now there are many more and the facilities for girls are much better."

Leeds boxer Nicola Adams became the first female boxer to win a gold medal at the Olympics. Her triumph came at the 2012 Games in London, and Nicola also won Gold at the 2016 Olympics in Rio.

"My first Yorkshire memory would be when I was five or six and I can recall my first visit to Roundhay Park in Leeds. We saw all the fish at Tropical World with my mum and dad. We'd play in the park and have an ice cream. I can also remember going to Temple Newsam where you've got those nice woods. I can still remember my first fight as a 13 year old. It was at East Leeds Working Men's Club and I boxed three one and a half minute rounds. I was inspired to take up boxing after watching a recording of the Rumble in the Jungle, that great fight in 1974 between Muhammad Ali and George Foreman."

Nicola Adams

Julian Norton

Vet Julian Norton: Well known on television because of the Yorkshire Vet series on Channel 5. Originally, he practised at the same vet's in Thirsk made famous by Alf Wight whose books were turned into All Creatures Great and Small.

"I was brought up in Castleford and lived in Lumley Street. I remember when my sister, Kate, was born in Pontefract Infirmary. I'd be about two and as a toddler I'd go to the home of my grandparents who lived near us. They had boarding kennels and kept a few pigs. I suppose contact with animals at that age set me on the path to becoming a vet.

"Some parts of Yorkshire have changed and some not at all. When I first started in Thirsk, we used to have 20 or 30 dairy farms, now we have two or three in the practice's area. Beef cattle numbers are dramatically down and similarly with sheep. Most people living in the Thirsk area are now not directly connected with farming whereas 20 years ago probably most were."

The selection gives a flavour of the My Yorkshire interviews, but there were many others.

One of the key points about the personalities, whether they are landed aristocracy like the 8th Earl of Harewood, footballers Norman Hunter or Billy Sharp, a businessman such as Irving Weaver (Strata Homes and owner of Harrogate Town Football Club) and musicians David Hartley from the Huddersfield Choral Society or David Hill, director of the Leeds Philharmonic Society, was their willingness to chat enthusiastically which is not always the case when public figures are approached by the media.

For instance, David Lascelles, the Earl of Harewood (pronounced Harwood) and a great grandson of George the Fifth, was most keen that I understood the correct pronunciation not only of his title but also of the family surname, Lascelles.

"It's Lascelles as in tassels," he reminded me as he put on the coffee before sitting down for the interview.

Norman Hunter, the legendary Leeds United footballer from the 60s and 70s who died of coronavirus in April 2020, may well have been a ruthless defender on the pitch, but in the comfort of his own home, he put you at ease immediately.

"You're the first journalist I've met who's been on time for an interview," was his opening remark on arrival for my appointment.

As I write, Norman's club are being revived by the Argentinian manager, Marcelo Bielsa, and playing a style of football in keeping with the club's illustrious past. Bielsa will be remembered as the coach who transformed Leeds' fortunes, winning promotion to the Premier League after an absence of 16 years in July 2020. He left Leeds in February 2022.

A My Yorkshire feature that took you back several generations to the periods when the region dominated the textile trade was with Adam Hainsworth, a director of AW Hainsworth, the famous textile company based in Pudsey near Leeds. The firm was founded in 1783 and its cloth was used to make the red uniforms worn by British soldiers at the battle of Waterloo in 1815.

Our interview was conducted before the retirement of the then Archbishop of York, John Sentamu. Hainsworth, a committed church goer and capitalist, explained the points he'd make to the Archbishop during an imaginary dinner.

"I'd talk to him about economics because as a country we have lost sight of wealth creation. I'd explain what wealth creation is and how important it is. How to turn 10 pence into a pound. You have to create wealth to generate taxes and to make it a fairer society. I'd also tell the Archbishop that people are unaware of the tsunami that comes with the level of debt the country is in."

Adam Hainsworth was referring to the state of the economy in May 2018, and if he thought the position was bad then, you can imagine his views in 2020 as the UK was struggling to cope with the Covid 19 pandemic forcing the Boris Johnson government to borrow billions of pounds keep businesses afloat.

CHAPTER EIGHTEEN

AND A FEW EXTRAS

As a journalist at the BBC and Yorkshire Television, I was fortunate that my natural interest in politics had been used professionally as I met several national politicians.

Covering cricket for The Sunday Times took me to Trent Bridge to report on Nottinghamshire's games in the County Championship; among the county's members and a keen supporter was the then Home Secretary, Ken Clarke, and a Nottingham MP. A popular visitor to Yorkshire Television, like Denis Healey, Clarke enjoyed watching cricket and, thankfully, had a life outside politics and appeared not to be obsessed with devouring all the paper work put in red boxes of Cabinet Ministers.

On one particular Saturday, the cricket had not produced any angles that required putting into the intros of any of the editions, so it was a struggle to write worthwhile copy. A wander around the splendid Trent Bridge pavilion gave you some ideas as you looked at the row of old bats and the black and white photos of Nottinghamshire teams featuring Harold Larwood and Bill Voce, but then something or rather someone more contemporary appeared.

The Home Secretary shuffled in and I thought a word with him, however brief, might help any creative thinking I possessed.

"Mr Clarke, I 'm covering the game for The Sunday Times. Any chance of a quick word on the cricket?"

"Please don't mention in the paper that I've been at the cricket. I'm supposed to be fighting crime."

As it happened, I did mention that the Home Secretary had been a spectator, but, like everyone else, had probably been bored by what he'd seen. Mr Clarke's presence made a line or two, and as the summer was drawing to a close, I reported that it wouldn't be long until he'd be watching Nottingham Forest playing football at the City Ground nearby.

Clarke was privileged to watch Forest because the team, then managed by Brian Clough, were one of the most successful and entertaining sides in England. Clough's achievements at Forest, a First Division championship, successive European Cup trophies and five times winner of the League Cup, were memorable, not least because Forest broke the stranglehold of Liverpool and had been a mediocre provincial club until transformed by Clough's charisma and unorthodox management style.

Brian Clough –
Nottingham Forest Manager
1975-93 and winner of consecutive
European Cups 1979 and 1980

His triumphs in the League Cup were naturally newsworthy and although Forest were not part of Yorkshire Television's editorial area, they became so in the late 1970s when Clough brought his squad to Scarborough to prepare for a League Cup Final replay.

YTV worked closely with ITV Sport which wanted an interview with Clough for their Saturday lunchtime football show. It was made clear to me that my brief was to speak to Clough and no one else.

Story ideas in London sometimes don't match the facts on the ground, and after filming Forest and Clough at a training session on the beach at Scarborough, Clough told the press he wouldn't be doing any interviews, but Peter Taylor, his assistant, would chat to the media in the Forest hotel.

As far as I was concerned, that attitude and offer were of little help because ITV would not be satisfied with a Taylor interview only. So when I spotted Clough in the hotel lobby, I asked him again if I could have a word.

"I've told you already that I'm not saying anything. Peter's doing the interviews."

With that, the most quotable manager of his generation, a national television personality and the people's choice to become the next England coach, walked towards the lift and got in.

I followed him and stepped into the lift as well. Clough wasn't best pleased.

"Young man, you're a persistent bugger. You can fuck off out of my lift. I've told you I'm not speaking to the press."

I did as I was told, and spoke later to ITV Sport to tell them of Clough's response. Inevitably, the story which they broadcast was an interview with Peter Taylor who may not have been as amusing as his boss, but he spoke with just as much football intelligence.

Thoughtful conversations on sport, in this case cricket, were, more often than not, the result of any meeting with Brian Close, the former England, Yorkshire and Somerset captain. A highly talented all-rounder, Close was one of the best and most successful skippers in Yorkshire's history between 1963 and 1970, winning four Championships titles and two trophies at Lord's in the Gillette Cup.

A lovely man, who liked a fag or two, the odd bet on the horses and a drop of whiskey, Close, I found, was a great help to reporters. A schoolboy hero of mine, I could never have imagined that in the future our paths would cross frequently as a television journalist and reporter for The Cricket Paper.

Rock hard on the field, Closey was warm and kind in other settings. After doing a story with him at a pro-am golf tournament in York, one of my first at Yorkshire Television, we met again in unusual circumstances a few weeks later, in a traffic jam in Hull.

I'd been stuck in a queue for least 30 minutes and started checking in the driver's mirror above my head to see who was behind, I noticed a bald head and a figure with thick eyebrows. That's Brian Close, I thought.

I got out and tapped on the window of Close's car.

"Now then. What brings you here?"

I told him I was the Hull reporter for Yorkshire Television and hoping to drive the story back to Leeds.

"Well, you can do me favour. Somerset (1971-77) have given me a benefit. I've got some ties and brochures in the boot. Do you fancy some stuff?"

Closey opened the lid of the boot which was full of boxes containing brochures and many dark red ties embroidered with the crests of England, Yorkshire and Somerset. Normally, benefit items are sold at lunches or dinners, but not in a traffic jam on the main road out of Hull.

Closey wanted £10.00, fair enough, so I wrote a cheque out on the roof of his car, and the tie and booklet, well-illustrated with pictures of his long career, remain treasured possessions.

Our next meetings were in far more conventional places, lunches, dinners, his home in Baildon, at Headingley or at an office in Leeds where he tried to sell me life assurance.

Because of his stature and thorough knowledge of cricket, Brian Close was the natural choice to turn to on many issues once he retired. In 2013, Yorkshire celebrated the 150th anniversary of their foundation at a meeting in a Sheffield hotel in 1863.

The Cricket Paper were keen to mark such an important event with a long feature in which I sought the opinions of Close and Ray Illingworth, another distinguished England captain who also led Yorkshire and Leicestershire. They were asked to produce the best Yorkshire teams they'd grown up with, knew of and played with.

Ray Illingworth and Brian Close former Yorkshire and England captains

I arranged to meet Close at Hollins Hall Hotel near Baildon, a venue he knew well and where he was well known. Our meeting developed into a comic scene that would have graced a sitcom.

Before we talked about the team he'd chosen, Brian was enjoying a cigarette near the entrance and once inside we ordered coffee and bacon sandwiches.

Against all the hotel rules, Closey lit up again and as we sat chatting, the waitress arrived and politely asked Brian to put his fag out. We then waited for our coffee, but as soon as the waitress turned her back, Close dived under the table and relit his cigarette. Smoke was drifting upwards and causing a bit of a stink once the coffee and bacon sandwiches were delivered.

"Mr Close. Please put out your cigarette. Smoking is not allowed inside."

Brian rose to his feet from under the table and apologised. Selection of his top Yorkshire eleven of all time began, and for the next hour or so, not another fag was lit, and in case you are wondering if Geoff Boycott was selected, the answer is no. Close chose Herbert Sutcliffe and Len Hutton as his best ever Yorkshire opening bats. Not many would disagree, but Boycott didn't make the final eleven, a choice that many would disagree with.

A natural liking for politics attracted me to journalism and in later life made it possible to teach the subject to newspaper and broadcast journalism trainees at Darlington College.

Teaching Public Affairs meant putting across the importance of the main components in central and local government, so that journalists would be able to handle confidently stories with MPs, Cabinet Ministers, Opposition leaders, councillors and senior local authority employees. Trainees also needed to understand the significance of the European Union and its institutions.

Arranging visiting speakers who were right at the centre of events, both local and national, was a regular method used to bring to life a subject that many trainees found a shade tiresome.

A frequent and much liked visitor to Darlington was John Burton, the Labour agent in Sedgefield, and then the County Durham constituency held by Tony Blair, Prime Minister from 1997 to 2007.

One of Blair's closest advisers and responsible for ensuring his selection as Labour's candidate for Sedgefield in the 1983 general election, Burton was warm and genial and always ready to help young journalists. All his talks were off the record, but in broad terms he excelled in explaining the pressure Blair faced because of his clashes with leadership rival Gordon Brown, the Chancellor of the Exchequer.

John Burton – Labour agent in Tony Blair's Sedgefield constituency

"I've seen the two of them walk past each other in a corridor at Downing Street and not acknowledge one another. Tony could never sack Gordon because he was too powerful."

Burton stressed, too, how vital to a proper functioning administration was the 24 hour Downing Street media office run by Blair's director of communications, Alistair Campbell, one of the most influential figures in Blair's government.

"These days Prime Ministers and Ministers have to be ready or their press officers have to be ready to respond at a minute's notice to unfolding events when the news cycle in 24 hours a day."

One of Burton's best stories concerned the build-up to the visit by President George W Bush to Blair's constituency in November 2003.

Hundreds of armed US security agents were on duty in Trimdon, where Blair had a home, as Bush and his wife were entertained by the Prime Minister and his wife Cherie.

During the visit, it was scheduled that Bush would have a cup of tea made by John Burton's wife, Lily. Burton's home in Trimdon was examined in minute detail by White House security agents, including the tea pot that Lily would use.

Just to make sure that Bush and his wife Laura would not be poisoned, Lily was instructed also to show the tea she intended to put in the pot. Not only that, the president's food taster sampled a brew and to the relief of John and Lily, it was passed as 100 per cent safe for Bush to drink in a day or two.

Burton, full of North East common sense, was an enthusiastic supporter of New Labour and the style and policies which Blair and Brown pursued to ensure victory at the polls. Burton, too, played a crucial role in continuing Blair's approach by putting in power younger politicians who backed New Labour.

With his profound knowledge of how New Labour operated in the North East and his sympathetic contacts, he'd been asked to look to the future with regard to who would lead the Labour Party following Brown, Blair's natural successor.

Well before Brown took over from Blair, I remember asking Burton whom he thought would be the long term leader of his party.

"You'll have not heard of him, but I tell you my job is to find a safe Labour seat for a fellow called David Miliband. You won't know him but he's very bright and is now Tony's Head of Policy at Downing Street.

"David will do the job till 2001 and then hopefully he'll be in the Commons. I'll be persuading David Clark, the MP for South Shields, to accept a peerage and then David can fight the seat.

"After a bit, he'll be made a junior Minister, then a Minister of State and then promoted to the Cabinet."

And that's precisely what happened; indeed, Miliband rose quickly and became Foreign Secretary from 2007 to 2010. Miliband's chances though of being elected Labour leader and his ambition to reach Downing Street were ruined by his brother, Ed, who also fought for the Labour leadership following Brown's resignation after losing the May 2010 general election.

Blair's and Burton's plans for David Miliband to take over the leadership and with it New Labour were wrecked by the election of his brother in September 2010. Within a few years, David had disappeared from UK politics, almost as quickly as he'd risen, and chose instead to live and work in New York where he ran a refugee charity.

Miliband was very much in the mould of the Labour politicians most closely associated with New Labour; other than Blair and Brown, Peter Mandelson notably played a prominent role. Appointed by Neil Kinnock, the former Labour leader, in 1985 to the influential post of the party's Director of Communications, Mandelson's media skills and the ruthless manner in which he operated, transformed the image of his party.

Peter Mandelson

Personally and professionally allied to Blair, Mandelson relished his function as Labour's spin doctor. Known nationally in the press as the Prince of Darkness, his power in the party not only grew, but was feared by many who loathed his methods. Elected MP for Hartlepool in 1992, the future Labour Cabinet Minister and European Commissioner for Trade, was high on my list of potential visiting speakers.

Mandelson's talk coincided with a visit to his constituency which is close to Darlington. His polished manners and dress sense were impeccable as we met at Darlington station. I've never forgotten his opening remarks.

"Have you met Tony Blair? Let me introduce you."

"I hear you've invited Peter to talk to your students," said the future Prime Minister who'd travelled on the same train from King's Cross.

"John Burton tells me they are a good lot and ask some hard questions."

Blair was then driven to Sedgefield and I walked with and chatted to Mandelson. In the short drive to the college in my car, he asked me about my professional background, and when I said I'd worked at Yorkshire

Television as a reporter, Labour's Prince of Darkness, an ex-TV producer himself, lit up.

"You'll know so and so. That's excellent. I had no idea you had worked in television. Now tell me about your students and how long I've got to talk and please make sure I have a glass of hot water."

Mandelson's address oozed charm and, playing up to his audience, stressed the importance of provincial newspapers but ...

"The Labour Party is always at a big disadvantage when it comes to the national papers because they have a natural Tory bias and that makes it difficult for us to win elections."

That opinion may or may not be true, but any Conservative bias in the printed press was overcome by Blair who won three consecutive general elections in which Mandelson played a major part.

All the students, some of whom would be first time voters in the future, were impressed with Mandelson's professionalism and his approach to questions. His replies treated the younger generation as equals; no attempt was made to talk down to them.

His style created a favourable impact and while some of his views on the hostility of the media to Labour needed challenging, nevertheless one of the principal architects of New Labour made some converts.

Equally smooth was Alan Milburn, another Labour politician in the North East who rose to national prominence under Tony Blair. MP for Darlington from 1992 to 2010, Milburn too advocated and advanced New Labour policies, in particular as Secretary of State for Health between 1999 and 2003. He, too, was eager to talk to the college's journalism students.

Alan Milburn – Darlington MP and former Labour Health Secretary

Smartly dressed and with manicured finger nails, Milburn, I thought, combined successfully a hard edge with a style that sought to create an instant likeable personality. I remember an exchange with him as he arrived at the college before speaking to the students again.

"Good to see you again. I'll be with you in a minute. I'm expecting an urgent call from the Lord Chancellor, Charlie Falconer."

I felt, probably unfairly, Milburn was showing off, but having spoken to Falconer, he proceeded to talk openly to our trainees on the role of a Cabinet Minister and, especially, the problems facing the National Health Service. This was most helpful because the structure of the NHS and how it was paid for was part of the Public Affairs syllabus.

What did surprise me was how and why Milburn suddenly became so angry and sharp with one our female students who'd asked a pointed but reasonable question.

He accused of her of being rude; the tone of his reply upset her so much she burst into tears, not good publicity for a New Labour Cabinet Minister if the story had leaked. Milburn later apologised and, hopefully by now, his inquisitor has developed a thicker skin so that she's not easily offended by aggressive politicians.

As a journalist, it was inevitable that you met several Cabinet Ministers of the main parties from time to time from the mid-1970s into the early 1990s and then as a Public Affairs lecturer. In their dealings with me, fairly short and sweet, both Conservative and Labour Ministers were open and friendly. On reflection, the one whose ego, however quietly expressed which stood out was Milburn's. Clearly able, I thought he was fond of himself, and you could tell why his manner might upset colleagues and officials who were too sensitive. Milburn decided to cut short his political career, but continued to do invaluable work on how to increase social mobility for young people from disadvantaged backgrounds.

The outcome of the 2019 general election which produced a large majority for the Conservatives and Boris Johnson caused a political upheaval in the North East where the Conservatives captured Labour seats that the party had held for generations.

You can imagine the shock and disbelief that Tony Blair and John Burton felt when the former Labour Prime Minister's constituency, Sedgefield, fell to the Tories. Sedgefield was not alone.

Teaching trainee journalists the importance of Public Affairs produced the odd amusing incident. Trying to explain and understand the complexities of local government finance was a challenge for me and students who clearly preferred to be somewhere else.

One session coincided with an OFSTED inspection; it could not have been worse from my point of view. One Welsh trainee, who was employed by the Llanelli Star, thought the best way to prepare for a lecture on the council tax was to drink several pints at lunchtime. The result was predictable. Lewis fell asleep and started snoring, and despite my best efforts to wake him up, he carried on sleeping.

Not what you want when your expertise as a lecturer is being assessed by a self-important government inspector. Not only did she lack a sense of humour, but also took great pleasure in pointing out in her official report what she considered to be the poor standard of the lecture in her opinion…and the embarrassing fact that one of the students had fallen asleep because he was so bored.

She didn't realise he was pissed, and, unfortunately for me, her report made dismal reading but, thankfully, it rebounded; her comments contained several spelling mistakes, the worst being – one student was so board. Her comments were written in weak English which any news editor would have sent back demanding an instant rewrite.

Just as the inspector had piled in with her critical remarks, I did too by marking in red all the spelling errors. I sent my comments to the college principal. That particular OFSTED inspector didn't visit Darlington again.

Throughout my career as a journalist, humour has been a frequent companion. My experience is that colleagues in newsrooms relish good stories, the stranger the better, and it's remarkable how many stories you come across where people land themselves in circumstances provoking public ridicule.

For weeks at Yorkshire Television, I was the subject of much mickey taking because, it was claimed, that during a murder story I was covering in Lincoln, I asked the senior detective in charge of finding the killer… "How seriously injured was the dead man?"

I was convinced that I hadn't been so stupid, but colleagues were not impressed with my denials which persist to this day.

Silly humour also cropped up at home in Leeds when I was living in a flat on Harrogate Road in Moortown, a suburb in the north of the city.

My cleaning lady at one period was earning money to pay for her training as a speech therapist. Bright, attractive and inquisitive, Theresa, a keen supporter of Leeds rugby league club, noticed dozens of my rugby union programmes laid out on the lounge floor alongside my newspaper cutting books.

"Hope you don't mind, Guy, but I've been looking at your newspaper reports and match programmes. I see you write on rugby union for the papers. Are you a snob or what?"

"Certainly not. What makes you think that?"

"Well, my dad says rugby union folk are a bit stuck up and I'm not sure he'd want me working here if you were like that."

"You can tell your dad, I watch Leeds on Sundays at Headingley from time to time and I've been to Featherstone and Castleford as well."

A week later, Theresa returned.

"I've had a word with my dad. He says I can keep on coming here. He says you sound a good lad, and you can come home for tea and talk about rugby."

"Theresa, it'd be a pleasure. What does your dad do?"

"He's a master bricklayer, but he's also an Elvis Presley singer. He dresses up as Elvis and sings at a club in Kirkstall. He loves Elvis and is very good, and what's more, he wants to be put in his coffin wearing his Elvis white suit with all the tassels on. You should come out with me and my mates to hear him sing one night."

"Theresa, I'll do that as well. But before I do that, you'd better tell me where you live."

I wrote her address down and before she started hoovering, she added another piece of priceless information to make sure I'd get to the right house.

"When you get to the front of our house, you'll see some gates. Just press the button and they'll open to the sound of Elvis singing Jailhouse Rock. That's where we live."

All perfectly true, and it proves the point that whoever you meet, however briefly, they may have a story that you can chuckle about for years.

CHAPTER NINETEEN

REPORTING IN LOCKDOWN

Fear and death gripped the country throughout 2020 and much of 2021 as Covid-19 affected all our lives. With the pandemic spreading, my coverage of rugby union and Yorkshire cricket was widely disrupted.

Sport at all levels – whether professional or amateur – ground to a halt. The last rugby match I covered was at Doncaster Knights against Coventry in March 2020. Soon afterwards, all games in the Greene King IPA Championship, the professional league below the English Premiership, were cancelled until further notice – a huge financial blow to clubs.

So, in my case, instead of reporting on Championship rugby until the end of April or the beginning of May, I was forced to take an unplanned break from reporting. Newspapers had to adapt quickly to the pandemic. Journalists worked from home instead of in the newsroom. The quality of the output did not suffer, and the papers for which I wrote, The Yorkshire Post and The Rugby Paper, excelled in the absence of any live sport.

Features, following interviews on Zoom, flowed, and in my opinion, newspapers enjoyed a good pandemic in terms of their coverage in the most testing of circumstances. As Yorkshire does not have a rugby union club playing in the Premiership, the sport almost disappeared from the sports' pages of The Yorkshire Post, but once international games – played in empty stadiums – were permitted, match reports and news coverage reappeared.

The YP's stature grew steadily during the crisis under the committed and energetic leadership of editor James Mitchinson. The financial problems facing provincial papers, already serious, deteriorated. Journalists took pay cuts to help their papers survive, and referring to the YP and its magazine, I thought the quality of the contents was enhanced for those people who prefer reading a print version rather than going online.

Having said that, the online content was put together by the same production team and looked attractive. Although my match coverage of rugby ended in March, the effects of the pandemic on clubs were far-reaching as sources of income dried up. A prominent figure in Championship rugby, Steve Lloyd, one of the main financial backers at Doncaster Knights, played an influential role throughout in the affairs of the Championship during the crisis. As chairman of the Championship clubs, Lloyd pressed and pressed again their case in his dealings with the Rugby Football Union, the governing body.

Coverage of elite rugby in the national media inevitably concentrates on national teams and the major clubs in England such as Exeter Chiefs, Saracens, or Leicester Tigers, but the significance of Championship sides like Doncaster, Cornish Pirates, or Ealing Trailfinders, must be stressed as they develop players for the Premiership. In Steve Lloyd, they are fortunate to possess a forceful and sensible advocate.

As the Covid-19 epidemic gathered speed and the lockdown extended into spring and early summer of 2020, cricket's future was threatened at both club and national level. The England and Wales Cricket Board worked miracles to ensure that the national team prepared safely and lived in bio-secure settings so that international teams, West Indies, Pakistan, Ireland and Australia, were ready to travel to the UK and compete securely between July and September.

The ECB was, therefore, able to fulfil its broadcasting obligations whose incomes are so vital to the solvency of the sport. Like other journalists, I needed to change my working methods. Instead of meeting Yorkshire cricketers and coaches at Headingley, Scarborough, or York, where face to face interviews would be conducted and then written up for The Cricket Paper, stories were done on the phone because it was safer and easier for players to chat at home.

Yorkshire, in common with other counties, played its games in empty grounds. It was the same for England's Test matches. As a reporter, I was nevertheless kept busy by The Cricket Paper, but felt frustrated by having to do interviews at a distance. Person to person is by far the best method because in my experience you can achieve much more by meeting someone and interacting with him or her.

Yorkshire County Cricket Club, as explained earlier, has always been a source of important news since its formation in 1863, and the brief season of 2020 was no exception.

Azeem Rafiq
former Yorkshire cricketer who
accused county of racism

The biggest story, attracting much national publicity which I feel was highly damaging to Yorkshire, was the racist allegations made by a former player, Azeem Rafiq, who accused the club of being institutionally racist. According to Rafiq, who appeared in 160 games in all competitions between 2008 and 2018, including skippering the T20 side, he suffered so much racial abuse he contemplated committing suicide. For legal reasons, it is not possible to consider in detail Rafiq's allegations, but an inquiry was set up by Yorkshire to investigate his claims, and the former player later filed a legal complaint alleging direct discrimination and harassment on the grounds of race.

This crisis, by far the most serious in the club's long, and sometimes stormy, history, eventually resulted in the sacking of several members of staff, including the director of cricket, Martyn Moxon and the head coach, Andrew Gale. The chief executive, Mark Arthur, resigned and a new chairman, Lord Patel from Bradford, took over and drove the club in a new direction so that it could engage far more with the large Asian communities in West Yorkshire.

Many of the changes which Lord Patel introduced included the appointment of a new captain for the 2023 season, Shan Massood, the Pakistan international. The racism crisis caused no end of bitterness, acrimony and claim and counter-claim. Rafiq's stance was supported by sections of the media and by influential MPs who were, in my opinion, quick to jump to conclusions without knowing all the facts.

The treatment of Rafiq following publication of his racism allegations was periodically shocking and horrible.

The scandal produced countless twists and turns involving notable Yorkshire and England players such as Michael Vaughan, Matthew Hoggard and Tim Bresnan. The team-mate of Rafiq, Gary Ballance, who'd also played for England and was the centre of the allegations, issued a public apology which was accepted by Rafiq, but it was then announced in December 2022 that Ballance would be leaving the club.

Meanwhile, Lord Patel decided he'd had enough and revealed in January 2023 that he would be stepping down as chairman of Yorkshire at the AGM in March.

The pro-diversity changes he introduced were welcomed by the game's governing body, the England and Wales Cricket Board who then agreed to maintain Yorkshire's Test status vital financially.

My own view? When the story broke, it was handled in London by The Cricket Paper and not by me on the ground, and considering the scale of the allegations Yorkshire were accused of, the county's handling of the issue to begin with from a media perspective was next to useless. Therefore, not surprisingly, the coverage was one-sided.

As someone who'd known Martyn Moxon for four decades, rest assured there's not a racist thought in his mind, and I never thought Yorkshire County Cricket Club was institutionally racist.

If that had been the case, I remember thinking when the scandal broke, why would the England and Yorkshire leg-spinner, Adil Rashid, a friend of Rafiq's, remain at the club?

The other view is this: so many international stars from the West Indies, Pakistan, India and South Africa have represented the county since the great Indian Test batsman, Sachin Tendulkar, became Yorkshire's first overseas player in the early 1990s, and in my opinion, would not have done so if Yorkshire were a racist club.

However, since mass migration into West Yorkshire began in the 1950s, there can be no doubt that Yorkshire should have done far more to take advantage of the talent and natural enthusiasm for cricket among the ethnic minorities. Looking ahead, with more than 30 percent of the cricketers playing in the Bradford League, traditionally among the best in the UK from an Asian background, Yorkshire should not be short of talent capable of being successful in first class cricket.

On the field, Yorkshire didn't suffer from controversy, and while they didn't win the Bob Willis Trophy or the Vitality Blast (20 overs), promising individual performances with the future in mind were recorded. The outstanding batting display was produced by Dawid Malan who was signed by Yorkshire towards the end of 2019 from Middlesex, which he captained.

A left hander, Malan rose in December 2020 to become the number one batsman in the world in T20 cricket, and quickly demonstrated why he had been recruited. He scored a splendid 219 against Derbyshire in the Bob Willis Trophy at Headingley in August, showing the class, temperament and technique that had earned him 15 Test caps for England and a successful recall to the England T20 side in the 2020 season.

Dawid Malan

Shortly before his Yorkshire debut, Malan gave me an excellent interview for The Cricket Paper from his new home near Wetherby. Thoughtful, analytical and self-confident, Malan spoke intelligently about his ambitions and his new team-mates.

"What has really impressed is Yorkshire's work ethic. They train as hard as anyone I've seen. I really like their ambition and determination."

Able to assess quickly the quality of his new county's bowling attack, Malan said: "Yorkshire have a good stock of fast bowlers. Ben Coad is fantastic and Matt Fisher and Jordan Thompson have impressed me. My first thoughts are about scoring lots of runs and maybe my name will be in the hat to play for England again in red and white ball cricket."

The results of his move to Yorkshire have been rewarding personally. Malan's form with his new team fulfilled his aim of being picked again in international cricket. In the T20 series against Pakistan and Australia, he made 23, 54, 7, 66, 42 and 21, and then in South Africa before Christmas 2020, Malan's class punished the opposition with scores of 19, 55 and 99 not out. His glittering form in T20 earned Malan a lucrative contract in Australia's Big Bash with Hobart Hurricanes, but before his first game he needed to self-isolate because of the prevailing Covid restrictions.

Dawid Malan is very much a central figure in Yorkshire's drive for trophies – the County Championship has not been won since 2015 and the county's achievements in limited over competitions have been poor for a club with its long tradition of developing high class cricketers. They've never won the T20 competition and Yorkshire's last silverware in white ball cricket came as far back as 2002.

Articulate, driven and blessed with the right temperament, Malan's career at Headingley has started promisingly, and with his first class experience stretching to 2006, the county is expecting even more from him now the worst of the pandemic is behind us.

Malan's form in the England 50 overs ODI side has been pretty prolific as was seen in the one day series against South Africa in which he scored a century at Kimberley in February 2023.

With Yorkshire being relegated at the end of the 2022 season, his responsibilities in Yorkshire's batting order are now even more strenuous as collectively the team try to regain their place in Division One.

During Covid, with no spectators, cricket appeared unnatural; no longer was it possible to meet friends at games, enjoy a drink or two and talk of past matches, heroes from the past and the stars of the present, like England skipper Joe Root, all-rounder Ben Stokes and the explosive fast bowler Jofra Archer.

Cricket provides companionship and fellowship, and being prevented from attending matches because of the pandemic came as a devastating blow, particularly to those whose lives had been dominated by the sport.

The retired Test umpire, Dickie Bird, who lives near Barnsley and who celebrated his 90th birthday in April 2023, had been accustomed in retirement to watching Yorkshire's games home and away, often travelling with the team on its coach. A single man and, as he admits, married to cricket, the pandemic and the imposed restrictions could not have come at a worse time.

Dickie Bird at home in Barnsley

Instead of regular company and being with like-minded people, whether Yorkshire players or county members, Bird was forced into isolation, like thousands of others of a similar age.

Always happy to chat to the media, after many weeks in lockdown, I put together a feature with Dickie for The Cricketer magazine, published in August 2020. He explained how he was coping at his cottage in Staincross near Barnsley.

"I'm struggling on and I'm not allowed any visitors, so I've been in the house by myself for weeks and weeks. In fact, I went into isolation the week before it became official. I'm vulnerable because I had a stroke 10 years ago, so I've got a pacemaker.

"I've been staying in bed for a bit longer in the morning because you can't go out, and after my shower I do some exercises in the bathroom. Then, I move into the garden to do some running. I walk first, followed by a run for 20 yards, try some sprints, even at my age, walk again and then run for another 20 yards.

"The gardener says I've worn away the grass with all the laps I've been doing. I've done exercises all my life because as an umpire I felt if I was physically fit, I was mentally fit.

"I'm pretty fit for 87. Regarding food, my neighbours have been good, leaving meals on the doorstep. I'm not the best cook, so all I have to do is to warm the food up. But I've burnt a few pans and once almost set fire to the oven. Indeed, I've had to do some cooking for the first time in my life.

"I have been a bit lonely, but I've been by myself all my life because I've never married and gave my life to cricket. I've missed it badly. I'd have been at every home game each day.

"I've missed the company of the members, chatting in the Long Room at Headingley, and missed the company of the younger players and watching them in the nets before play starts.

"I never dreamt I wouldn't be going to Headingley, and when they talk about playing Tests with no spectators, for me umpiring would feel very strange because there'd be no atmosphere.

"To be honest, I've had loads of calls, and when I was 87 in April, both Dennis Lillee and Sir Richard Hadlee left me messages. I also had calls from India and the West Indies. Lillee was, in my opinion, the greatest fast bowler who ever lived. Bob Platt, who opened the Yorkshire bowling with Fred Trueman, has been on and that's always a good hour.

"I've watched lots of films which have kept me going and I've never eaten so many chocolate bars in my life. I must be going crackers but the good thing is that I've not put on any weight."

A national institution and a generous contributor to charity, Dickie Bird, certainly in the numerous phone calls I enjoyed with him during the Covid crisis, retained his sense of humour. He needed to because not only was he deprived of watching Yorkshire in the short season of 2020, but he was also prevented from going to Oakwell, the home of Barnsley Football Club which Dickie has supported all his life.

Cruelly, he suffered yet another blow before Christmas when his hopes of going away to Scarborough for a week during the festive season were ended. The hotel where Dickie had spent a pleasant and relaxing Christmas in normal times phoned to tell him it would be unsafe to come, so it was cancelling his booking.

As before, neighbours rallied round, cooking Dickie a Christmas dinner and other meals to cheer him up.

The lovely ground at Worcester where the city's cathedral presides over New Road is not surprisingly one of Dickie's favourite venues and, as with all counties, those spectators who have the time to watch Championship cricket (four days) tend to be retired for the most part.

Just before the first period of lockdown in March, while first class cricketers were preparing for what should have been the start of the 2020 season, a fascinating lady with a deep love and knowledge of cricket gave me the opportunity to write another feature for The Cricketer.

What appears to be the peaceful setting of New Road is a far cry from the hectic life led for many years by Cynthia Crawford, Margaret Thatcher's personal assistant, friend and confidante, during her period as Prime Minister. Indeed, Cynthia, now in her early 80s, went to live with Lady Thatcher in Belgravia until her death in April 2013.

As president of the Worcestershire Supporters' Association, Cynthia entertained her former boss at New Road on several occasions – a world away from the Falklands' War, the Miners' Strike, clashes with the EU and the poll tax riots – all of which Cynthia saw at close quarters during her time in Downing Street.

"The cricket was never on in Downing Street. Definitely not. I can't honestly say that Lady Thatcher was keen on cricket, but Denis Thatcher was and went to the Oval a lot. He and I talked much about cricket and I remember the England team visiting Downing Street soon after Mrs Thatcher became Prime Minister. I can see Bob Willis (former England skipper and fast bowler who died in December 2019) now towering over the PM and myself.

"When Sir Denis died in 2003, she came to Worcester three years running to stay with me and my husband. I brought her down to New Road and we sat in the Ladies' Pavilion and had a cup of tea and cake. Lady Thatcher enjoyed chatting and had lunch with the board. Everyone was delighted to see her and people made a fuss. She enjoyed the ambience of New Road because it's homely. She liked the views of the cathedral, she signed autographs and was glad to be out of London.

"I'm close friends with Graeme Hick (former England and Worcester batsman) and he came to our home in Worcester when Lady T was staying with us. We went out to dinner and I remember on one occasion, she and Graeme were sharing each other's dessert at the restaurant. Both were roaring with laughter.

"After Denis died, I moved in with her at her home in Belgravia and got Lady T to watch the cricket on the television. She turned to me and said, 'I like that player.' I replied: 'That's Brett Lee. He's from the opposition'. Do you remember when Lee had that bit of blond hair at the front? It was then and Lady T took to Brett Lee quite keenly."

At the time I was seeing Cynthia Crawford at New Road, I met again a former Yorkshire player, Kevin Sharp, who'd recently been appointed Head Coach at Worcestershire. Today's generation of England supporters may not be aware that Sharp, a talented left handed batsman who scored more

Cynthia Crawford –
Margaret Thatcher's personal assistant
at Worcestershire's cricket ground

than 13,000 runs for Yorkshire in first class and one day games between 1976-91, played a major role in the development of England captain Joe Root.

Sharp, before moving to Worcestershire, had coached at Yorkshire (2003-11) and first came across Root, then a highly promising schoolboy cricketer living in Sheffield, during his coaching career at Headingley.

As Sharp explains, he was impressed immediately with Root's ability and confidence.

"Joe was 12 or 13 and had just been awarded a Yorkshire scholarship which had been recommended by the youth coaches. I was having an intensive session with Anthony McGrath (former Yorkshire and England cricketer and now Essex coach) and unknown to me Joe had arrived early and was watching from the back of the indoor school.

"I had a chat with him and it was remarkable because straightaway he talked about cricket like an adult. I was thinking, 'This lad can talk a good game and you're going to be good if you can bat as well as you can talk.'

Kevin Sharp former Yorkshire batsman and later coach to Joe Root

"Joe was a little schoolboy, blond and angelic. I was excited and asked him what he wanted to do in the nets. Joe looked at me straight in the eyes and said, 'I want the same session as McGrath.'

"I'd been throwing a new ball at Anthony from eight yards and told Joe I couldn't do that because he would be hurt. He smiled and said he'd be OK. So I said 'you've asked for it' and told him to put on his equipment.

"I set a field for him and got a brand new ball and told Joe that he was going to get it. He smiled and just nodded. I ran in and threw this ball at him. It swung, he left it, left another one and then defended one. Joe had a really good technique and I thought this lad could play.

"I let him have a bouncer, Joe rocked back and it chipped his grille. I followed through and stared. Joe just smiled and then went home with his dad to Sheffield.

"Immediately, I went to see Ian Dews, the academy director, and told him that Joe Root would open the batting for Yorkshire one day. Ian said that was a big statement to make about such a young schoolboy. I continued to coach Joe right the way through and always felt he would make it."

As Root's progress grew, Sharp decided to pick him as a 15 year old for Yorkshire Seconds at Abbeydale Park where Joe played for Sheffield Collegiate.

"We were playing Derbyshire and I told him he'd be opening. Derbyshire had a lively attack who had all played first class cricket. They saw this little boy walk in and the bowlers smiled.

"They bowled short at Joe but he used the pace of the ball. He cut and pulled and hit a six over the sightscreen and got 57. I told him he'd done well but in the next match he'd be batting at six in the order because a senior player was back.

"Joe said, 'that's good because I can learn now how to play against spin.' He was really mature."

Joe Root batting for Yorkshire

As Joe's batting coach, Sharp knew that Root was ready to be introduced into the County Championship side in 2011, a season in which Root scored more than 900 runs in Division One, hitting one hundred and four fifties. Root had made his List A debut in 2009 and his first class debut the following year.

As Root has developed into one of England's best batsmen in the post war era and become a genuine world class star, alongside Steve Smith (Australia), Kane Williamson (New Zealand) and Virat Kolhi (India), Sharp points out that Joe has always kept in touch.

"Joe has good character and remembers people who've been supportive and played a part in his development. When he was 14, he said if he went on to play for England, he'd leave me two tickets on the gate at Lord's.

"So in July 2017, on his debut as England captain at Lord's against South Africa, Joe left me two tickets for me and my wife. We watched him and sat with his parents and grandparents. He went on to score 190.

"You always knew that Joe was up for the fight, he relished pressure and that for me is a sign of a potentially great player. The more responsibility you give him, the more Joe thrives on it. That is a sign of someone who is special and the ones who make it are the strongest mentally."

As the Covid crisis deepened and the death toll in the UK passed more than 120,000 towards the end of February 2021, Joe Root's batting in the two Tests against Sri Lanka at Galle momentarily cheered up millions of sports fans.

The England captain's performances – 228 in the First Test followed by 186 in the Second – were a timely and much needed morale booster for a nation struggling against despondency and the pandemic.

Root's smile and superb innings took us away, however briefly, from the misery of winter and encouraged us look forward with hope to happier, and more normal times in the summer.

The Yorkshireman scored more than 400 runs in Sri Lanka and, as a result, strengthened his position as England's captain and his status as the team's outstanding batter.

As Root flew to India to play in his 100th Test, following his triumphs in Galle, he had become the fourth highest run scorer in Tests for England, overtaking the illustrious David Gower, Kevin Pietersen and Sir Geoffrey Boycott.

Now, with more than 10,000 runs in Tests and 28 centuries by the end of the 2022 summer, Root goes from strength to strength and is easily England's most reliable bat.

In fact, Covid and the restrictions imposed on the England players made little difference to Root, certainly when it came to scoring runs in Tests.

Indeed, he thrived so much so that Wisden Cricketers' Almanack, in recognition of the 1,708 runs he scored for England in 2021, anointed the Yorkshire batsman as the Leading Cricketer in the World in its 2022 edition.

Gradually, the stress of being England captain in 64 Tests, especially after the total failure of the team in the Ashes series in Australia in 2021-22 during which they were thrashed 4-0, brought about his resignation in the spring of 2022, but thankfully, Root chose to continue playing Test cricket.

Arguably, Root, who always looks relaxed at the crease, will now build on his superb reputation as he concentrates solely on batting, his mind freed from worrying about team selections and fielding and bowling changes.

Without the anxiety of being captain and following the appointment of his successor, Ben Stokes, Root put together a run-spree which set up wins against New Zealand and India.

At Lord's he scored 115 and this was followed by another Test hundred at Trent Bridge(176) and in front of his own supporters at Headingley, he made 86 not out out. Root's form remarkably continued at Edgbaston where India suffered as his timing, shot selection and placement of the ball and, indeed, quick scoring compiled 142.

By the end of the 2022 season, Root's record was truly outstanding 124 Tests, more than 10,000 runs at an average of 50.00 and 28 Test hundreds.

This excellent record was to grow even more impressive, so by the end of the Ashes series in the summer of 2023, Joe Root had made 11,416 runs in 135 Tests, scoring 30 hundreds and no doubt more on the way in his next series in India between January and March 2024.

CHAPTER TWENTY

AND FINALLY ...

As cricket lovers know, both the 2022 season and the 2023 summer saw Joe Root at his best and most innovative, flicking the ball over the keeper's head with perfect timing to score boundaries, but what was also encouraging for the future of English cricket and Yorkshire, when he's available, was the confirmation that Harry Brook is a batsman of the highest quality.

His outstanding form in the County Championship in 2022-967 runs, three hundreds and six fifties at the scarcely believable average of 107.44, inevitably earned selection for the Test team, and while Brook was out cheaply on his debut against South Africa at the Oval in September, his class and talent exploded during the Test series in Pakistan in December.

Brook learned to play at the Burley-in-Wharfedale club near Ilkley and then at Sedbergh School where he benefited from the coaching and advice from the ex-Sussex and Durham professional, Martin Speight, with whom Harry is in regular contact. His temperament and skill adapted quickly to the dusty and flat wickets in Pakistan, and his feats in the three Tests were truly astonishing, consecutive hundreds in Rawalpindi (153 and 87), 108 at Multan and 111 at Karachi.

Brook's achievements, on top of winning the T20 World Cup at Melbourne against Pakistan in which he scored 20 invaluable runs, thrust him into the international spotlight, but sensibly his sudden fame thankfully didn't go to his head. Brook's success against Pakistan 468 runs at an average of 93, not surprisingly made him one of the most sought-after batsmen in the IPL auction. Yorkshire's rising star, the best young batsman in the county since Joe Root and Jonny Bairstow, was bought for £1.3 million.

As it turned out, apart from scoring a dazzling hundred for Hyderabad Sunrisers in only 55 balls, Brook's IPL experience was not the most productive, but the IPL and its expansion illustrates how cricket has changed dramatically since the eras mentioned earlier.

Can you imagine how much Don Bradman would have earned in the IPL and for that matter Harold Larwood and Fred Trueman?

Brook, the perfect example of the contemporary cricketer as he performs successfully in both red and white ball formats, has transformed his status, and on current form, is one of the top players in the world. Armed with a solid defence combined with a wide array of attacking shots, plus ambition and determination, he has overcome stressful periods and, indeed, was dropped by Yorkshire at one stage. It doesn't seem all that long ago that I went to Harrogate where he was playing for Yorkshire Seconds. Apart from his mature and calm attitude displayed when he was being interviewed for The Cricket Paper, I can also remember the thoroughness he showed.

Brook made the point that soon after he was dismissed, he wrote down in a notebook how he got out, so that, hopefully, any error would not be repeated. His attention to detail has brought its rewards. His Yorkshire team-mates, good judges of character and talent, noticed Brook had the technique required to establish himself in first class cricket at Chelmsford against Essex in 2018. In Yorkshire's second innings, 19-year-old Harry set up the county's win with 124, his first hundred in the Championship and as Bairstow said of a superb innings: "The way he played through mid-off and through the covers was special."

Capable of adjusting the tempo of his batting to match circumstances, rather like Root and Bairstow, Brook scores quickly in all formats. Whether he's playing in Tests, ODIs, T20 or for the Northern Superchargers in The Hundred, Harry has made and is making a substantial impact in a sport which is now reflecting the speed of modern society. In the world of social media, Brook's contemporary, but given his background in Wharfedale and the Howgill Fells surrounding Sedbergh, he's been moulded by the North of England where life can be less hurried. Harry's family too will ensure he's not carried way by fame and riches as he plans to establish a Test reputation that ranks with the best.

Brook's character and technique seem to fit the revolutionary approach of England's coach, Brendon McCullum and skipper Ben Stokes. While it can be argued that Brook's method in Bazball was certainly careless at times during the Ashes, his innings of 75 at Headingley and then 85 at the Oval where England levelled the series at 2-2, unquestionably his batting in the Third and Fifth Tests contributed to England's wins.

With the end of the Ashes at the end of July 2023, in which Harry scored 363 runs (av 40.33), he had completed a brilliant start to his Test career, and at only 24, this Yorkshire batsman can look forward to his future and add to his 1181 runs (av 62.15)achieved after only 12 Test matches.

Harry Brook

I'd kept in touch with Brook throughout the Ashes and once the series had finished, he fulfilled an earlier promise to do a story for The Cricket Paper. His reflections on the Ashes were fascinating.

"I think I had a good series and put in some vital performances which helped us to get a few wins, but I was disappointed not to get a big score. As regards Bazball, our aim is to put pressure on the bowlers by being positive rather than being stupid or reckless.

"You have to find the right balance between not being daft and our aggressive method. I would rather be out driving and then nicking off than being out playing a defensive shot. Batting at Headingley was a dream come true for me and the Leeds Test(July 6th to 10th) was one of the personal highlights.

"I had at least 10 of my family and friends in the ground. The Ashes as a whole was the best fun I've had in cricket. Both Ben Stokes and Brendon McCullum are super-chilled. You can do whatever you want to be positive. You rock up and crack on. I can assure you there's method behind the madness, and now I know that England can handle the pressure situations better than we did. We know how to absorb the pressure and then when to put the foot back down.

"I thought we were unlucky not to come away with a series win. The last three Tests at Headingley, Old Trafford and the Oval showed how good we were. We were entertaining, more people are coming to watch Test cricket, Tests are a great day out, the atmosphere is pumping, and England are helping to secure the future of Test cricket."

While Brook's Test career is a success story that Yorkshire can be proud of, the county's achievements in rugby union during my time as a reporter have seldom matched those achieved by our cricketers. Earlier, Rotherham's distinction of becoming the first Yorkshire club to be promoted to the Premiership was discussed, and for a time it seemed that Leeds were close to establishing themselves at the highest level.

Indeed, I covered their home games at Headingley regularly for The Sun, clearly football drove the paper's sports' coverage, but Test rugby, the European competitions and the Premiership were reported thoroughly. My space allocated by The Sun's highly professional sports desk was normally 16 paragraphs which would be slashed to seven when you read the paper on Mondays. Interestingly, following my first report for The Sun, the then sports editor answered my phone call to check that my copy was satisfactory.

In common with other teams in the Premiership, Leeds' opponents contained some overseas players whose names required careful spelling. I remember the conversation only too well with the sports editor.

"You're the new lad. I see that your copy mentions Samoans, Tongans and New Zealanders. Are you certain that you've got their names right?"

"Yes, I am."

"We'll be in touch next week."

I was then in my fifties and no longer a lad, but I understood the importance of accuracy. I mentioned this conversation to a colleague who'd held senior positions at the Evening Post in Leeds, a well-respected journalist who was working with a prominent news agency in Leeds that supplied stories and features to the red tops. His thoughts were quite chilling.

"If you'd got one name wrong, you'd never have worked for The Sun again. It's a paper with the best professional standards."

Happily, I continued to be employed by The Sun as a freelance until Leeds were relegated from the Premiership in 2011, having been promoted first in 2001 under coach Phil Davies, the former Wales international, who was a pleasure to deal with. Phil's commitment to the goal of turning Leeds into a permanent member of the Premiership was evident; his enthusiasm and endless hard work shone continuously, qualities that took Leeds into the Heineken Cup, the best European competition. Leeds also won the Powergen Cup against Bath at Twickenham in 2005, but the progress on and off the field could not be sustained, despite super stars such as All Blacks' scrum half, Justin Marshall and South African centre Andre Snyman.

It can also be argued that Stuart Lancaster, a future England coach who was to forge an outstanding reputation at Leinster, the powerhouse of Irish rugby, developed his coaching and man-management skills at Leeds. As Lancaster, now in charge at Racing 92 in Paris, entered the coaching system with England in 2003, he was succeeded by Neil Back and Andy Key. Sadly, Back, a World Cup winner with England in 2003, and Key, also ex-Leicester Tigers, were unable to deliver the consistency needed to keep Leeds in the Premiership.

Since relegation, the club has been in gradual decline, falling out of the Championship and National One and as the 2023-24 season began, Leeds were competing in National League 2 North alongside Rotherham Titans. Currently, Yorkshire's ambitions to put out a competitive team in the Premiership rely on Doncaster Knights, based at Castle Park in Armthorpe. Financed by businessmen Steve Lloyd and Tony De Mulder, whose generosity and singlemindedness has built a stadium of Premiership standards, the Knights are one of the most feared clubs in the Championship and the only full-time professional club in Yorkshire.

A well-run outfit which attracts players with the potential in the long term to appear in the Premiership, Doncaster, whether under coach Clive Griffiths or Steve Boden, taking over from Clive, are not only ambitious, but sensibly keen to develop their own players through the club's academy. Writing for The Rugby Paper or The Yorkshire Post, Doncaster's progress through the leagues has provided me with plenty of opportunity to cover a club which is proud of its Yorkshire roots and one which plays a style of rugby that should be supported at Castle Park by many more spectators than the 1200-1500 who regularly attend home games.

Clive Griffiths

Steve Boden

Doncaster Knights work hard in the community, promote themselves enthusiastically and provide top class facilities for dozens of kids to learn and enjoy the game. The 2022-23 season was not a league campaign in which the Knights fulfilled their potential. A sixth position, 10 wins and 12 defeats, represented a failure if you judge their efforts by the previous season. The highlights for me as a reporter were Doncaster's victories, home and away, against Ealing Trailfinders, by any standards one of the biggest spenders in British rugby.

Financed by Mike Gooley, the brains behind the success of the travel agency, the London club have spent several millions of pounds on players, coaches, analysts and facilities with the aim of earning promotion to the Premiership. So far, despite vast expense and the Premiership's hostility to promotion from the Championship unless that league's winner meets promotion criteria, Ealing Trailfinders remain in the second tier.

Therefore, considering their on-field strength, they won the Championship in 2021-22. Doncaster's triumphs in beating Ealing twice in the league were undoubtedly one of the genuine, remarkable moments in their history since being founded in 1875. So with Doncaster able to retain several of the squad who participated in that league success, it was surprising that this notable achievement could not be repeated in the 2022-23 season. Declining form and injuries resulted in them dropping from second to sixth, and seeing Jersey Reds clinch the Championship; often the team's performances made uncomfortable watching for the Knights' coaches and in particular for Director of Rugby, Steve Boden, who frequently looked drained of energy at the end of a league match.

Yorkshire's tradition of producing international players is distinguished; in my time as a reporter, for example, Sir Ian McGeechan (Headingley, Scotland and the British and Irish Lions), Peter Winterbottom (Headingley, Harlequins, England and the Lions), Mike Harrison (Wakefield and England), John Spencer (Headingley, England and the Lions), Rob Andrew from Middlesbrough who played for England and the Lions, Mike Tindall from Otley who won the World Cup in 2003 and played for Bath and Gloucester and more recently, Danny Care who plays for Quins and England having started at West Park in Bramhope in Leeds and then at Otley.

With almost 100 clubs affiliated to the Yorkshire RFU and a population of more than five million, plus many prosperous firms as potential sponsors, the foundations have been in place and are for a substantial Premiership club. Neverthelss, both Rotherham and Leeds both failed, so it is now the responsibility of Doncaster Knights to try to earn promotion and then in the long term they can be judged against the best clubs in England, like Saracens, Exeter Chiefs and Leicester.

As the 2023-24 rugby season began to unfold, simultaneously the UK's political parties were preparing for a general election to be held no later than January 24th, 2025. In the late summer of 2023, Labour led by Sir Keir Starmer were comfortably in front in the opinion polls, suggesting that the Conservatives and the Prime Minister Rishi Sunak would lose power.

Yorkshire over many decades, and since the Second World War ended, has attracted politicians who achieved national status; indeed, Sunak is MP for Richmond, having succeeded William Hague from Rotherham, the former leader of the Tories and an ex-Foreign Secretary.

On the Labour side too, significant figures of international importance have made an impact. Hugh Gaitskell, Labour leader from 1955-63, was a Leeds MP, much loved locally and highly respected nationally. Harold Wilson who took over from Gaitskell following his early and tragic death at only 56 was famously from Huddersfield and twice Prime Minister. Others too. Denis Healey as was seen earlier was Chancellor of the Exchequer and Defence Secretary in the late 1960s and 1970s. Educated at Bradford Grammar School, Healey was a Leeds MP for 40 years and because of his genial personality was as popular in the boardroom as he was in workingmen's clubs.

Barbara Castle mustn't be forgotten; educated in Bradford and then became Transport Secretary and Employment Secretary under Wilson. Less well known is perhaps Merlyn Rees, another Leeds MP, who served as Northern Ireland Secretary and later as Home Secretary from 1976 to 79. When it comes to the present generation of Labour politicians who can be expected to be appointed to the Cabinet are Rachel Reeves, MP for Leeds West since 2010, and Yvette Cooper, MP for Normanton, Pontefract and Castleford, first elected in 1997.

Writing for The Yorkshire Post magazine's My Yorkshire feature I had the opportunity to interview both Reeves, the Shadow Chancellor, and Cooper whose experience as a Cabinet Minister in Gordon Brown's administration from 2007 to 2010 should be considered a big advantage bearing in mind how few Labour front benchers have served in a Cabinet.

Reeves, I liked immediately: welcoming, thoughtful and clearly on top of her brief. She's a politician who has, I believe, sold herself and Labour to big business which may have doubted the ability of a Labour government to run the UK economy efficiently. Who knows, Rachel Reeves could well become the first female Labour Prime Minister if the political winds blow favourably in her direction.

Cooper, the Shadow Home Secretary when we met at her office in Castleford in August 2023, is similarly sharp but much more familiar with how Whitehall works than Reeves. Easy to talk to and

Rachel Reeves MP

well prepared for the My Yorkshire story, Cooper's knowledge of how the system operates equips her for the challenges of the Home Office, and in her case, as in Reeves', Yorkshire's voters and the national media will be observing keenly how they cope with the stressful demands of high office, assuming Labour win power.

Observation, examining politicians critically and holding those in power to account is one of the major functions in a democracy of the media, a free press being vital. Journalism, in its conventional style, newspapers and broadcasting or in the digital and internet age, is changing rapidly, but its purpose to report accurately in a straightforward and easy to understand way remains the same.

Yvette Cooper MP

I'm proud to be a reporter and while you have the odd regret, I've never covered an Olympics, World Cups in cricket or rugby or written daily for a national paper, I've done stories and features with many sportsmen and women who have achieved distinction internationally, both in the past and currently. I've loved Yorkshire cricket since I was a schoolboy living in Honley near Huddersfield and have therefore gained so much pleasure dealing professionally with Sir Len Hutton, Sir Geoffrey Boycott, Fred Trueman, Brian Close, Dickie Bird and Ray Illingworth. The latter was always so thoughtful and methodical and, in my experience, you always came away with a decent story because Illingworth was so knowledgeable and blunt.

Martyn Moxon, the former Yorkshire and England batsman, was regularly helpful when he was in charge of Yorkshire cricket; in fact, I don't think I've come across a more decent man in professional cricket and it was so wrong that he, along with several other employees at the club, were brutally sacked as Yorkshire were accused of being institutionally racist, in my opinion, a wild allegation.

Cricket and rugby union have been kind to me as a journalist as indeed has the Yorkshire media, but you can only do so much without the cooperation of people at the centre of the story in happy and bad times, and I can honestly say that Yorkshire folk, from all backgrounds, have made my professional life a genuine pleasure.

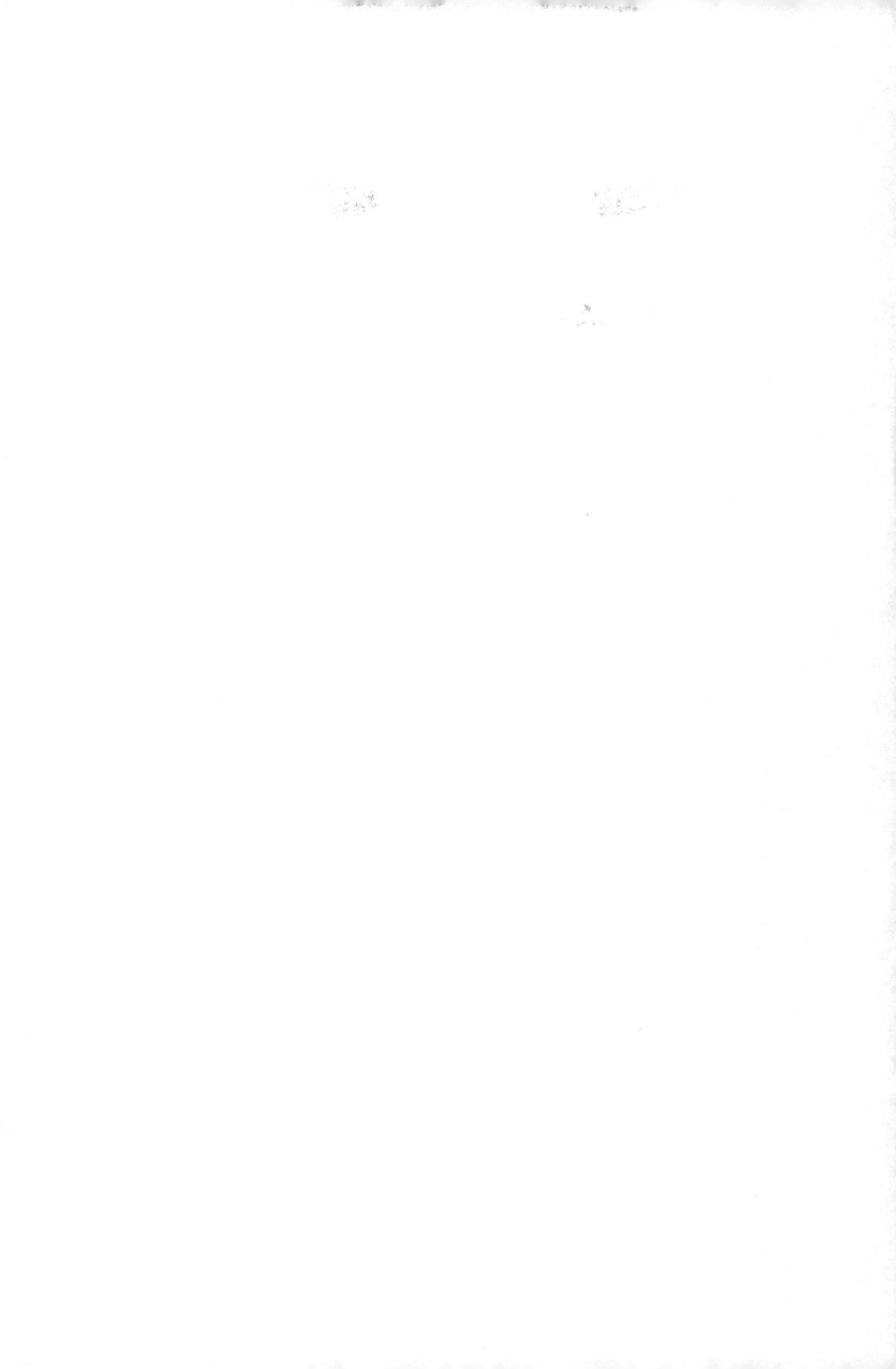